THE STORM

MARKETS MEET MOTHER NATURE

The Storm: Markets Meet Mother Nature

ISBN: 979-8-9950304-0-9 Paperback

ISBN: 979-8-9950304-1-6 Ebook

THE STORM

MARKETS MEET MOTHER NATURE

BY

BILL BYMEL

Dedicated to Mom

Mary Bymel would've turned 86 on the
day this book releases

And to My Children

Elizabeth, William, and Philip whose future
this book may impact

And to Peace and Love for All Humans

CONTENTS

Weathering a Perfect Storm

Growing up in tropical South Florida in the 1980s, I witnessed examples of the power of Mother Nature. As a teenager sweltering in August of 1992, my family fled our ranch-style house just a few miles from Fort Lauderdale Beach as Hurricane Andrew barreled toward us on a direct, unforgiving path toward our home. We were one family of thousands who evacuated on a moment's notice. We went inland to a friend's house in Plantation Acres because they had a generator, a critical, lifesaving, and often rare energy source those days. If you've ever lived through a major hurricane, you know the forces I speak of. There's an eerie quiet before the storm as pressure drops in the region and all senses are piqued: a cacophony of intense winds that rage powerful enough to knock down walls, the sights of objects too heavy to fly just floating by like a feather, and an intense feeling of dread. It all adds up to remind us of forces more powerful than anything humans could conquer.

Andrew took a last-minute turn south, sparing my family home from a direct hit, but it caused catastrophic damage to our area, especially in Miami and the surrounding communities to the south. The storm literally wiped away entire subdivisions like matchsticks and obliterated decades' worth of construction, possessions, and history within a matter of hours. I remember volunteering in Homestead and Florida City for weeks, handing out water and food to middle-class families— just like mine –reeling because they lost everything. It was called a "once-in-a-hundred-year storm." And for many years after that, life seemed calm again. Florida rebuilt while facing a different kind of storm known as the 2008 Great Financial Crisis.

Survivors of hurricanes, folks who require rescue physically or financially: they're the ones who talked themselves out of evacuating, certain that history immunized them from future threat. Some lost everything. Others lost their lives. They all said the same thing: "I knew it was coming. I just didn't think it would be this bad."

Thirty years later, I find myself watching a different kind of storm gather—one that won't arrive on a single catastrophic night, but rather through a slow-motion convergence that's already underway. This storm doesn't have a name or a category rating. The National Weather Service won't track it. But make no mistake: It is coming, and most people are responding exactly like those neighbors who stayed behind during Andrew in '92. We see the warning signs. We acknowledge the risks. But we convince ourselves it won't be that bad and that the systems we've built are strong enough to withstand what's ahead.

Our past does inform our future—unless we let it blind us. This book is about the future, not the past. That means any predictions we make may not come true. You will read my perspective on what the future may look like based upon cycles that have repeated themselves on Earth since before recorded history of Human Being.

We are standing at the convergence of three powerful forces impacting society: huge debt loads coming due at the end of a prolonged period of cheap money, dramatic societal paradigm shifts accelerated by a pandemic and an aging population, and the increasingly undeniable impacts of climate volatility and regular catastrophic events. These forces do not merely coexist— they amplify one another like warm water fuels a hurricane, creating a scenario that can blindside citizens and leaders, in only what can be described as a perfect financial storm.

Throughout history, civilizations have risen and fallen based on their ability to adapt. The Romans built aqueducts and roads—yet crumbled. Kodak dominated photography for a century—until digital killed it. The British Empire's sun set. Institutions that seemed unassailable vanished when conditions shifted.

These historical examples aren't merely interesting anecdotes. They represent a fundamental truth that we ignore at our peril: everything moves in cycles. This is the essence of Mother Nature. What goes up, eventually comes down. When I speak of Mother Nature in this book, I am referring, not only to the big, beautiful planet we inhabit and all the amazing creatures we live amongst, but I am also referring to mother nature in its theoretical form, a reference to the cyclical nature of all things in the universe.

This book explores how these cycles—economic, technological, societal, demographic, and environmental—interact and what their convergence means for our financial future. But this is not a book of doom and gloom. Storms, while destructive, also clear away what's unsustainable to make room for what comes next. For those who understand the patterns and prepare accordingly, storms create unprecedented opportunities.

I've spent decades in real estate and finance, witnessing firsthand how markets rise and fall, how trends emerge and dissipate, how seemingly solid institutions can dissolve when foundations shift. My experiences have taught me that the ability to recognize patterns—to see the storm forming before others do—is the most valuable skill in navigating financial uncertainty.

In the pages that follow, we'll examine how market cycles work and why we're due for a significant correction. We'll explore how societal transformation is reshaping where and how we live and work. We'll confront the real economic impacts of climate change, particularly on insurance, property taxes, and real estate construction costs. We'll dissect common fallacies that keep us locked in outdated thinking. We'll examine what the aging of the Baby Boom generation means for housing, wealth transfer, and supply. And most importantly, we'll discuss practical approaches for not just surviving but thriving in the months and years ahead.

In this book, you'll learn not just to survive the storm, but to emerge stronger. The wind is picking up. The barometer is falling. Clouds are gathering. Time to prepare for The Storm.

I.

UNDERSTANDING THE STORM

CHAPTER 1

The Value of History

"History doesn't repeat itself, but it often rhymes."
- MARK TWAIN

The Roman Empire: Modern Society's First Lesson

Admittedly, history was not my thing as a kid. My parents and teachers proclaimed that history informs our future, but that piece of wisdom never rang true for me at the time. Growing up in the late 20th-century America as a middle-income kid with an abundance of American technology and opportunity available, what could I possibly gain from guys communicating on stone tablets? In our natural state, children and young adults think they know everything. The older I got, I realized how little I do know. During my egotistical 20s, I developed a vision for what my life should be. My "should" was a vastly different plan—aspirational, untethered, fueled by big dreams of becoming a movie producer or screenplay writer. In my twenties, I believed the future was something you built from scratch, that sheer will and vision were enough to shape whatever life I wanted. History? That was for academics. I had no use for looking backward when I was so busy racing forward.

Now, I want to be clear about something. I don't believe history should cloud or limit our actions. The past is not a cage and treating it like one is its own kind of trap. The value of history isn't in letting it dictate what we can or cannot do—it's in being a compass. The patterns are there for anyone willing to study them. And once I started looking, I couldn't stop. I became fascinated by the predictable cycles that repeat across centuries and civilizations—the way empires rise on the same ambitions and fall into the same blind spots, the way markets inflate and correct with almost rhythmic precision. If I could read those cycles, I realized, I might be one step ahead of where everyone else was looking.

That curiosity eventually pulled me deeper, past market charts, into the ancient world itself. I started to wonder: what was it like to be a Roman two thousand years ago, living at the imperial high-water mark of a civilization unlike anything the world had seen? What struck me most—those Romans had no idea they were living in "history." To them, it was simply life. A very present life. Their roads, aqueducts, and armies—this was progress, perhaps even permanence. They looked at their world the way we look at ours: as the pinnacle, the best humanity could ever offer. Their technology felt advanced, maybe even indestructible. And yet, from where we stand now, it was so primitive. They couldn't see what was coming. Only a few centuries later, their empire would lie in ruins, and the very people walking those marble streets have no framework for imagining that collapse. The Romans looked at their present the way we look at ours—convinced it would last.

That is the real lesson history offers. Not just the facts of what happened, but the reminder that every era believes it is the exception. Every civilization assumes its moment is the summit. The Romans did. Don't we?

Obviously, the Romans didn't have technology the way we think of it today. But as any history-crazed 6th-grader will tell you, Roman engineering was just as groundbreaking and life-changing as our modern technological inventions -- as much as the Internet or iPhone. The Romans created aqueducts to harness water as an energy source to power mills and mines. They experimented with new agricultural methods, including irrigation and crop rotation, and they invented a sewage system to remove waste and provide clean drinking water. The Romans built stone and concrete buildings, bridges, and roads, allowing for both the movement of goods between cities and towns and greater connectivity among civilians. News and gossip spread as quickly as items could be transported, and the military had unprecedented access to far-flung locales, allowing them to gobble up land and grow the Empire's resources. Relics of these innovative systems and feats of architecture remain today in Rome's many famous fountains, at the Colosseum (AD 80), and the Forum (8th Century BC -- AD 608). Recognize how these technological feats seem so mundane to us in a 21st century modern culture. Will there be museums about the internet someday?

Had I been paying attention in grade school, I would have learned that the Roman Empire's many notable engineering innovations and inventions were equally matched by its sophisticated and complex financial achievements. Not only did it develop banking, lending, investment, legal, and taxation systems, but it also introduced a standard currency that enhanced a vast international trade network and generated significant wealth for industrious individuals and the government. This economic surplus allowed the Empire to invest in the previously mentioned infrastructure (buildings, bridges, roads, clean water, waste removal) that led to long-term prosperity and stability.

The Romans, as we all know from our history lessons, were unable to hang onto their Empire forever. Eventually and gradually, the mighty civilization crumbled. Though the exact reasons are still being debated, several factors factually contributed to its demise, many of them economic. The Empire faced issues with overspending and overexpansion, inflation, high taxes, and a decline in trade and agricultural output. There was political instability due to corruption and greed. Mounting external threats and a military spread too thin, drained of resources and weakened a once-dominant culture, leading to its decline and eventual demise. Mother Nature played its role as well, burying the great city of Pompeii in 79 AD. Even a civilization so advanced had a major blind spot when it came to the power of volcanic eruptions.

Societal life cycles mimic the seasons we see in nature. Just as Mother Earth gives us the mildness of springtime to plant and nurture our seeds, the warmth of summer for them to grow, and the cooler temperatures of autumn for the harvest, eventually, whatever grows will wither and die. The remnants lie fallow under winter's chilly blanket of snow and ice, gathering energy and nutrients for new growth.

Anything that is born eventually expires and creates space for a new thing to be born. This is true of seasonal plants, animals (recall the dinosaurs), empires, organizations, and economies. Humans eventually return to earth: ashes to ashes, dust to dust. The ebb and flow of life is ever prevalent and cyclical. Societal shifts and economic shifts share this common thread. Through all of Earth's cycle, one constant resource has always existed. It has stayed ever present as an asset for humans to use and fight over for millennia: LAND!

Land (real estate) has always played a significant role in any economy. Vast amounts of the wealth of nations were built on the production of landowners. It's the only asset on Earth that never goes away, fixed in place, can be reused, is limited and finite in number, and historically has retained value. The entire measure of the early empires was based on the amount of land captured and controlled. Land provides additional value with natural resources such as oil and gas, or land can be fertile, used to farm crops or animals.

In fact, if one pauses to consider the longevity of modern cultures and how much land ownership has played a pivotal role in creating wealth for multiple generations, then a case can be made that real estate has the longest history of value retention comparable to any asset class (perhaps gold?). Whether it be for business purpose use, geopolitical control, or simple shelter needs, real estate is literally a home base of all economics, pun intended.

Kodak & Ford: Case Studies in Organizational Lifespans

One certain fact of history is that, as any organization (or Empire) grows larger, they become less nimble, less accepting of change, more difficult to effectuate pivots when necessary. These lessons have played out repeatedly in modern American business.

Let's explore the extraordinary lifecycle of Kodak, a long-standing blue-chip company that remains the darling of professional and amateur photographers alike. George Eastman had a dream to make photography accessible to the masses. From the company headquarters in Rochester, NY, he released his first camera, appropriately called the Kodak No. 1 in 1888, to wide acclaim.

For nearly a century, Kodak experienced a steady rise in popularity through consistent innovation and the development of new products such as the Brownie camera (1900), the first 8mm amateur motion picture camera (1932), color film (1935), and the Instamatic (1963, 1972). By staffing up with a fleet of elite scientists and chemists, the company continued its growth trajectory by expanding into lithium batteries, high-tech film processing, slide projectors, and even pharmaceuticals. Kodak was there when Commander Neil Armstrong and Buzz Aldrin landed on the moon in 1969. Astronauts carried a proprietary Kodak stereo camera to record the event and broadcast their lunar landing to the world.

By the 1980s, Kodak was the Roman Empire of the film world. It controlled 90% of the film and camera market in the United States, and annual sales had reached $10 billion. The company reached its peak just as it came under threat from a new technology: digital.

Ironically, one of Kodak's own engineers, Steven Sasson, invented the first digital camera in 1976, but executives at Kodak failed to capitalize on its potential. They believed film would continue to dominate. Competitors such as Sony, Canon, and Nikon seized the digital opportunity and ran with it. By the early 2000s, Kodak's stock sank below $10 a share and in 2012, the company filed for Chapter 11, facing over $6 billion in debt. Kodak's failure to adapt quickly enough to the digital revolution was one reason for its downfall, but it's also true that almost all great companies follow this pattern. Though Kodak is widely recognized as a pioneer in its field and still exists in a diminished state—like the ancient fountains fed by aqueduct technology in modern-day Rome—it is far from its glory days of the 1980s.

I detail the high-level events of Kodak's rise and fall because numerous great companies cycle through a similar pattern. The only core difference is how long the cycle takes. When a company is on the rise, gathering wealth and power, it is better positioned to take risks. Once it reaches its peak, it tends to slow down, becomes mired in bureaucracy, and stays safe, comfortable instead of adapting. Often, it faces external threats and must divert resources to protect its position. Sometimes, companies can reinvent themselves from the ashes of a decline phase. And other times, they simply become an historical footnote.

One such company that has famously bounced back from death (more than once) is Ford Motor Company. With $28,000 in investor seed money, Henry Ford launched the Model A automobile in 1903. He was almost broke by the time the car hit the market but turned a profit within months. Shortly thereafter, in 1908, the Model T car was released, which sold 15 million units over a 20-year time span and was praised for its durability, efficiency, and affordability. These characteristics were important to buyers because what they'd been getting around on previously was horses: creatures that were expensive to purchase, to maintain, and not terribly reliable or efficient.

Aside from disrupting a centuries-old horse market, Henry Ford also revolutionized mass production at a relatively low cost through the introduction of the assembly line method. But he didn't stop there. In 1914, Ford made an unprecedented managerial decision to reduce shift times from 9 hours to 8 and double his factory worker's pay to $5 a day, which had tremendously positive ripple effects: his own employees could afford to buy the product they made on the line. An increase in retention, productivity, and profits further boosted the bottom line. Ford Motor Company peaked quickly---within just two decades---and became one of the largest and most profitable companies in the world.

By the late 1920s, competition was nipping at Ford's heels. General Motors and Chrysler were racing to market with newer designs and models with more bells and whistles. Ford stubbornly refused to deviate from his prized Model T, and then the Great Depression hit (the recession of all recessions). It was a dark time in America, and the company failed to adapt. Talk of bankruptcy continued until after WWII as Ford suffered from quality control issues, lack of access to resources, and continued pressure from competition, both foreign and domestic.

A valiant restructuring effort was launched in the 1980s, which brought the floundering company back from the brink of death. It rolled out popular trucks and SUVs that stabilized operations until the Great Financial Crisis of 2008 (the "GFC"), which then brought the company to its knees once again. Ford was hurting badly in the early 2000s. Under new leadership of Alan Mulally, former CEO of Boeing, the company returned to its visionary roots and committed to building affordable and reliable cars and trucks. Ford remains on top to this day, demonstrating that even a company with a solid foundation is subject to market volatility, societal changes, and the cyclical nature of organizational growth and decline, which brings us to the current state of the American economy.

Real Estate Cycles Through the Eyes of a Florida Kid

The phases of any economic market cycle mimic those found in organizational lifecycles, societal prosperity, nature, human life, and history. Whether we choose to call those phases "accumulation, markup, distribution, and downturn"/ "expansion, peak, contraction, and trough"/ or "introduction, growth, maturity, and decline," any economy and every society is generally operating in one of those four phases and in that order.

Whatever phase of life the overall economy is in, so too is the real estate market. The two are intricately intertwined and inside of any economic cycle, asset classes such as real estate can have their own multiple phases based on demographics, population migration, and new economic opportunity. As we've explored with the Roman Empire, Kodak, and Ford Motor Company, when a business or economic cycle is in decline, a new business, innovation, or opportunity will spring out of it. Who will step forward to challenge tech giants such as NVIDIA someday and when will that happen?

The people I consider my mentors, who are 20 or more years my senior, give credit to the Savings & Loan bank failures of the 1980s-90s with providing new, once-in-a-lifetime opportunities for them. Most self-made real estate millionaires and billionaires I know attribute their greatest wins to deals that emerged when old institutions crumbled.

A perfect example of this is the creation of Ocwen Financial Group, which was founded by a friend (his name is Bill too), and Ocwen (now named Onity Group) is a leading non-bank mortgage servicing company in the USA. The Ocwen founders built a business by acquiring failing bank thrifts that owned both commercial and residential real estate mortgage loan portfolios and recognizing that a servicing firm was needed to manage those assets. When banks failed and lenders disappeared in 2008, Ocwen was perfectly situated to capitalize, creating multiple businesses to support the huge volume of distressed debt that needed resolution: this kind of ingenuity and resourcefulness happens all the time during more volatile market cycles. Fun fact: the name Ocwen was derived from NEWCO spelled backwards. Bill admits often that he and his co-founders lacked much creativity.

Before I get too far ahead, allow me to provide a little backstory about myself. Born in Chicago in the 1970s, I'm a Floridian at heart. My family moved to South Florida when I was just a few months old. At the time, Fort Lauderdale was relatively small, around 700,000 population, mostly known as a tourist-centric Spring Break destination---the ideal environment for a boy who liked to fish and lived a short bike ride from the beach.

Florida has always had a boom-and-bust real estate culture, which I had a front-row seat to because my dad was a residential real estate broker. After we moved there, starting in the 80s, the area churned through several cycles, and each followed a similar boom and bust pattern, resulting from various twists of the general economy.

The Boom-and-Bust nature of Florida far pre-dates me. In the early 1900s pre-Depression, Henry Flagler, a founder of Standard Oil, began to invest heavily in Florida's infrastructure. He extended the Florida East Coast Railway from St. Augustine to Miami, which opened the area to development and tourism. People were able to easily travel to and around an area that had previously been inaccessible. Flagler built a string of luxury resorts along the coast, including the Breakers in Palm Beach, creating a desirable winter destination for elite families from the northeast. Flagler also invested in several significant commercial real estate development projects, which attracted residents and businesses and spurred tremendous growth. He was a key figure in the early 20th-century boom economy in Florida, and his name is plastered on streets and building everywhere. Flagler's investment drew flocks of families to Florida, some for vacation, many more permanently. Several real estate bubbles busted in the earlier 1900s, several instigated by con men and companies who sold swamp land to unsuspecting Americans using the hype of Florida's promise.

South Florida, like every other corner of the U.S., was rocked by the Depression. Real estate went bust, property values plummeted, vacancies skyrocketed at newly constructed hotels and commercial buildings. Population declined when people left the area to look for work as tourism dried up. Despite FDR's New Deal efforts, South Florida suffered a deep dry spell until it was revitalized once again by the economic growth spawned out of

WWII: increased manufacturing and wartime production, military training and spending, agricultural expansion, and a rebound in tourism. Notice the cause-and-effect pattern that starts to develop as we explore. It's not so easy to predict or recognize cause when it's happening, but there is always an effect down the road that can be tied to one or more causes, as time will tell.

By the mid-to-late 80s, Fort Lauderdale and Miami were heading toward another downward spiral. Due to over-construction, the condominium market imploded with rising interest rates. I witnessed that collapse as a youngster and then witnessed another rise in real estate values in the late 90s, early 2000s, just as I started my real estate career as a fix and flip investor and broker.

Having watched Dad roll with the market tides, I was drawn to real estate because it is a fundamental investment class. Buying a home is at the core of the American dream, and it's a hard asset that (theoretically) never goes away. Historically, owning land was a sign of royalty and power. And today, owning a home is still a steppingstone to building wealth.

Real estate was a consistent place to be at the time I got into it, with 5% to 7% annual appreciation most of my life. In the early 2000s things were easier. One almost couldn't make a bad investment, not dissimilar to how real estate prices rose from 2012-2022, in the years since the bottom of the Great Financial Crisis. Anyone with a heartbeat and a little bit of brains can make money as long as the value of an asset is on the rise and interest rates remained stable or low.

Though my father was not an investor, he and others in the industry who had been through previous economic and real estate cycles, trained me to understand that appreciation in the double digits, over 10%, was an indication that something was amiss. Dad always said, "Anyone can make money in up times." Like the wind, if the markets are at your back, then it's very easy to pick winners from losers, even if you don't always make the right decisions. But when the market starts to bubble, and everything---no matter what it is---starts rising in value, it may be a sign of trouble. When the bubble bursts, that is what separates the adults from the children in the room. One of the key elements I've noticed in asset bubbles about to burst, is when investors factor appreciation into their modeling decisions.

Real estate itself, particularly in Florida, is highly localized by nature. By local, I don't mean cities, counties, or even towns. It's localized block-to-block. There are properties in certain areas where you wouldn't feel safe walking at night that sell for the same price as properties that are listed just a few blocks away in gated communities. When those two demographic prices start to conflate, that's another sign of a bubble, and one of the reasons I stopped buying in 2006. As an adult student of history, I was seeing trends and market clues. No deals made sense in 2006-2007, not dissimilar to today.

In 2008, the bubble was caused by cheap financing available to all types of residential speculators and loan originators willing to approve anyone to feed the system. Whether you were an investor or an owner occupant, you could obtain any mortgage just for being alive, and that access to virtually free capital with low credit standards was the primary cause of the housing bubble burst in 2008. Lenders and Bond Managers were to blame, and the mortgage industry will never be the same. As I am friends with many cohorts in the world of securitization and other lender friendly leverage facilities, I can't speak too poorly of those who created the storm that crashed our housing market in 2008. It amazes me that not one person was ever indicted or held accountable for poor practices. I guess you can't send an entire ratings firm to jail, but you could fine them. Just like con men of pre-depression who sold swamp land to Americans from boiler rooms, the causation of 2008 evolved from a lack of proper oversight or guard rails on the free market.

We're seeing the same trend develop now as we did back then: deregulation, overvaluation, and huge appreciation. Single-family home values surged from 2020 through 2025, and even where appreciation cooled by late 2025, affordability remained badly strained. Residential prices have stayed elevated regardless of the condition or quality of the asset. It's become increasingly challenging to find, buy, or rent decent property in America, a clue that some systemic failure may be looming.

Defenders of today's real estate market say, "Not to worry! We have plenty of equity and high standards for credit," which is true for a good portion of the owner-occupied Fannie Mae loans. However, there remains a ton of alternative credit out there, originated based on artificial and overinflated value of the asset and not on the borrower's credit.

What is the cause of the inflation in the real estate market? This time around, the primary reason is the extended run on cheap capital and the now forgone chance for people to lock in a 3-4% mortgage rate on their homes. Institutional investors, including the banks, were able to borrow dollars from the federal government---i.e., from the U.S. taxpayer---at zero interest for over a decade and then go out and loan that money at 3-5%. Now that banks can no longer borrow money at zero interest, they must figure out how to make money.

Home ownership is the cherry on top of the American Dream, and at least half of the real estate market is owned by individual people who invested for the sole purpose of building personal equity. But when you look at real estate from a business perspective, it's purely a numbers game. Can your tenants pay you enough to cover the property maintenance costs and the mortgage *and* provide you with a profit?

In other words, what is the cost of owning that return on capital? What is the principal and the interest? Look at the hard costs, all of which are going up due to inflation. On a multi-tenant building, hard costs include property management expenses such as landscape and infrastructure, common areas, garbage removal, snow clearing, etcetera. In the case of commercial properties, tenants often bear the burden of insurance and taxes when they sign triple net leases. In most states, taxes are directly related to the value a city or county attaches to property assets, which, as we know, are much higher than their true value.

In keeping with historical perspective, there are a few key assumptions to retain when considering real estate value. First, the historical CAP rate expectations in commercial or residential investments are going to trend in comparison to the cost of whatever the "safe bet" is our society. For us now, and hopefully for the rest of my life, the US Dollar and Treasury notes have been the standard. The risk premium of owning and managing real estate can vary from very little to 10% or more and is positively correlated to Treasuries.

All this to say that anyone who invested in multi-family low rise housing in the Southeast at a 4-5% CAP, where these assets were selling in 2021-22, you've probably had most of your equity wiped out. Why would anyone want to buy a C-grade apartment complex and deal with all the headaches, only to make less than you could if you were to buy a government bond?

As we approach the end of the real estate market's maturation phase, especially in mortgage financing, it becomes important to consider the numerous direct and ancillary industries that will feel the ripple effects of any impending decline in production or asset value. Think about all the people who make their living from real estate:

- Residential brokers, agents, and owners
- Commercial brokers, agents, and owners
- Mortgage lenders, servicers, and brokers
- Investors
- Lawyers
- Appraisers
- Developers
- Architects
- Engineers
- Inspectors
- Market research analysts
- Builders and general contractors
- Title companies
- Valuation companies
- Property management companies
- Cleaning companies and landscapers
- Food and beverage groups
- Planning and zoning agencies
- Tech companies such as Zillow, OpenDoor, Trulia, auction.com, etc.
- Online banking companies such as QuickenLoans, SoFi Financial, Capital One, etc.
- Fixtures and appliance manufacturers
- Materials Suppliers (flooring, cabinets, windows, furniture),
- Day laborers and heavy equipment suppliers
- Interior designers and cleaners...all the way down to the kitchen sink!

Given the vast number of people and tradesman involved in the real estate and mortgage businesses, any large-scale disruption in the market is likely to affect everyone. A major devaluation of commercial real estate can snowball if landlords and banks go bankrupt. It's already happened since the interest rate shift. If you were a customer of Silicon Valley Bank or First City Bank in Florida, you woke up one morning, and your bank no longer existed. Without getting into a detailed analysis of why these banks failed, the important takeaway is that the writing is on the wall. These examples act like foreshocks in a trembling market.

Embrace Cyclical Thinking

The U.S. economy has held strong for nearly eighteen years since the Great Financial Crisis of 2008. That's a record-breaking run in the grand scheme of things. It's quite easy to get caught up believing that the winning streak will last forever, but such is not the case. Nothing can last forever, and it's safe to say we peaked at the end of the era of cheap money in America.

We have a choice as to how we will handle the gathering storm of decline. We can panic and run through the streets screaming, "The sky is falling! The storm is coming!" or lock in. The reality is, through every market downturn or recession, it is the outliers who have become the most successful---the people (and companies) who are willing to think outside the box and shift with societal changes and market tides.

I've come to experience that if we are aware of any decline, we can spot the opportunities that others tend to overlook, and we can be the outliers. It's all a matter of context.

When Michael Jordan was at the top of his game for the Chicago Bulls in the 90s, gathering trophies and championship titles like gumballs, he went home to watch and rewatch the tape of the game he'd just won. He performed this routine not to pick apart his or his teammates' flaws but to search for the one element of his game that might be missing. He was looking for one small adjustment that could be added. Like a chef trying to perfect a recipe, Jordan was always looking for ways he could improve. He wasn't blind to changing conditions on the court, with his team, with management, or within the overall umbrella of the NBA. The requirements for success evolve and change over time.

What worked in the past may not work today or tomorrow. We must adjust and think outside the box, and this is what I request you to consider in the pages ahead. This is not a book about following trends, but it does trace trends that exist and provides guidance on how to stay ahead. Most importantly, this book is about awareness and leadership.

I'm someone who enjoys a good storm. Maybe it's because I grew up in Florida, and hurricane season was a chance to have school cancelled (the Florida version of "snow days"). When Hurricane Andrew arrived the summer before my senior year of high school, it wiped out a huge chunk of Miami and led to the introduction of new building codes.

While I sympathize with victims of Mother Nature's wrath, I do relish the power of a good thunderstorm. It reminds me that we are but tiny specks of dust on this whirling earth, and we are living on a planet that is beyond our control. Perhaps you will join my storm excitement as well. After the rains, a rainbow may form along with a pot of gold at one end.

The Roman Empire didn't fall in a day. Kodak spent decades in decline. Ford has survived near-death twice. Real estate markets have boomed and busted for centuries. Every cycle in this chapter followed a predictable pattern: rise, peak, decline, and renewal. The survivors were those who recognized which phase they were in and adjusted accordingly. But here's what makes our current moment unprecedented: we're not facing a single cycle reaching its natural conclusion. We're facing multiple cycles—financial, environmental, demographic, technological—all cresting simultaneously. The real estate market is maturing at the same time climate volatility is rendering traditional risk models obsolete. Banking deregulation is rising just as the cost of capital resets after seventeen years of artificial suppression. Work patterns are shifting while insurance markets are collapsing in the very regions that drove growth for the past two decades. Any one of these cycles would demand our attention. Together, they create something we haven't seen before: a perfect storm where the failure of one system accelerates the collapse of the others. Understanding individual cycles isn't enough anymore. We need to understand what happens when they converge.

CHAPTER 2

Debunking Fallacies

"Believe nothing, no matter where you read it or who has said it, not even if I have said it, unless it agrees with your own reason and your own common sense."

- BUDDHA

A fallacy is a plausible-sounding idea built on false premises—an unsubstantiated assertion delivered with enough conviction to pass for fact. A misinformed impression hardens into consensus, and that consensus becomes "true" for most people. The internet is full of them.

I bring your attention to this word because, in today's culture, where we're bombarded with so much information (and misinformation) from so many directions, it's quite easy to get caught up in what the masses say. And that's how fallacies grow.

Fallacies are dangerous because they limit our perspectives and perpetuate complacency versus proactive thinking or approaches to virtually every area of our lives, including our careers, sociological norms, and economic trends, all of which are driven by how and where we get our information. Inside the uber-tech social media environment within which we all now exist, fallacies (of all kinds) grow and spread faster than ever before.

I was in college when the Internet first became mainstream in the early 90s. Like many other kids in their 20s, I saw it as a means of finding the truth. Initially, it seemed to be a forum where facts could not be hidden. Instead, over time, it has evolved into an abundance of channels and forums where people share or receive their own set of opinions, ideas, and perspectives, which are commonly misconstrued as facts or truths. It has become a dumping ground for different points of view and a vehicle for the creation, provocation, and promotion of fallacies.

Let's examine some fallacies that have shaped financial behavior for decades.

A Woman's Place Is in the Home

One of the most famous and limiting fallacies was that a woman's place is in the home. This notion is a remnant of 19th-century gender roles that promoted the idea that women belonged in the private domestic sphere while men belonged in the public sphere of politics, business, economic, social, and cultural activity. An outdated stereotype that has survived despite women securing the right to vote in 1920, the Equal Rights Amendment of 1923, the Equal Pay Act of 1963, Roe v. Wade in 1973, Madeline Albright's appointment as the first female secretary of state in 1997, and many subsequent milestones, women's quest to bust out of the traditional confines of the "home" are still very much alive today.

The politics of gender equality aside, I was fortunate enough to grow up in a household surrounded by strong-minded, independent, savvy women. My mother was the first person in her family to graduate from college. Instead of getting married in her early 20s, as her sisters did, she pursued a master's degree. Domestic work and child-rearing are among the toughest jobs out there, but my mother was not destined to focus her life in the "home". Her education, interests, and drive led her in a different direction.

When she married my dad, a man outside of the Catholic faith in which she'd been raised, he was 100% supportive of her choice to work full-time as a planned giving consultant for nonprofits and hospices throughout Florida. Though my dad worked in real estate and contributed in a big way to our household finances, Mom was the primary breadwinner.

Mom was one of a kind and didn't seem to mind one bit that she couldn't cook for shit. The entire family relied on her mother's famous chicken noodle soup, a recipe she picked up from the Jewish doctor she worked for in Milwaukee. My grandmother was a devout Roman Catholic who went to mass multiple times a week and was a firm believer in the fallacy that women belonged in the home. Though her ideals failed to land on her daughter's approach to life, the woman absolutely mastered perfect schmaltzy, savory, deeply memorable chicken soup that could not be replicated. I still miss it to this day. When my mom attempted to recreate the recipe after her mother died, she butchered it.

Mom's success in her career, paled in comparison to my sister Suzan, who is a powerhouse talent manager. Frequently named to lists such as "Hollywood Reporter's Women in Entertainment Power 100," Suz is a passionate philanthropist known for her work with the United Nations, CARE, and EWM. Though she has not given birth to children of her own, Suzan has acted as a surrogate mother and godparent to stepchildren, actors, producers, writers, and other creatives, nurturing their careers and their sense of self.

I am so proud to have been raised in a socially conscious household and to be related to women who have busted the fallacy that they belong in the home. Sure, that's a great choice for women who want to be there, but for those who don't, thank you for breaking out of yesterday's thinking and forging new paths. The women wore the pants in my family.

The Gold Watch Fallacy

After World War II, in the 50s and 60s, many people believed US corporations offered job safety and financial security. Folks took jobs thought to have a long-term potential for advancement, stable income, health benefits, a retirement plan, and one day, a valuable gold watch. All you had to do is commit 40 years of devoted employment with one company or outfit, and employees expected to receive the proverbial gold watch and a pension.

WWII veterans returning from bloody European battlefields bought into the gold watch-pension promise. For some early subscribers, it worked. Job security equated to moderate financial stability, but as time wore on, the promise morphed into a fallacy or a gimmick to attract lifelong employees.

By the time I was a kid in the 1980s, a market cycle of boom to bust led to widespread layoffs. It took a few decades before pensions dried up. Many of the once-blue-chip companies went out of business and many employees saw pink slips instead of a watch.

Fast-forward to the present, post-Covid information age of remote freelance employment and independent entrepreneurship, and we're looking at a very different landscape. The gold watch fallacy now represents blind loyalty to behemoth corporations, a relic of our parent's generation's way of thinking. That shiny gold watch is viewed as a trap, a cheap and hollow means of employee enslavement to a single corporation.

Today's workforce is on the move. They're not going back to the office. They don't need to live in commuter suburbs of major urban areas to earn a decent salary, and this reality has severely altered commercial real estate. Even though executives and landlords may believe there will be a return to the office buildings of yesteryear, it will never get back to 100%. How does a permanent 10 or 20% occupancy reduction impact cities like New York, Miami, Atlanta, Austin, Chicago, Dallas, Los Angeles, and Seattle? We're about to find out.

The Zero-Sum Fallacy

The Zero-Sum fallacy is another outdated and incorrect assumption perpetuating the idea that one person's loss equates to another's gain at the expense of the loser. This concept is prevalent in economic theory, and its validity is widely debated. It also happens to be the exact opposite of my own personal philosophy that win-win solutions are always possible, no matter how dire the situation might seem.

My first book, *Win-Win Revolution*, explores that concept through the context of the secondary mortgage market. Written nearly a decade after the collapse of the subprime mortgage market in 2008, it focuses on various solutions that benefit both the lenders and the borrowers and reveals opportunities within the NPL sector, often overlooked by traditional investment strategists. There's always a creative, alternative solution to capitalizing on someone's misfortune.

Several other examples disprove the zero-sum fallacy, primarily one's job. You go to work, and you earn money. Sure, you lose your personal time, and the boss loses cash, but the wins cancel the losses out. Now, more than ever, society is focused on winners vs. losers, which makes me push back even harder against the zero-sum approach because it doesn't have to be that way. We certainly have leadership that believes America needs to win at all costs. It's not how I might lead the country, but it certainly is shaking up the world order. And that alone, may be good to shake some sense into modern markets.

The Interest Rate Fallacy

In 2002, Alan Greenspan, Chairman of the Federal Reserve, made a peculiar announcement at a Joint Economic Committee Meeting in Congress. Greenspan said:

"The ongoing strength in the housing market has raised concerns about the possible emergence of a bubble in home prices. However, the analogy often made to the building and bursting of a stock price bubble is imperfect... A home in Portland, Oregon, is not a close substitute for a home in Portland, Maine, and the 'national' housing market is better understood as a collection of small, local housing markets. Even if a bubble were to develop in a local market, it would not necessarily have implications for the nation as a whole... Because the turnover of homes is so much smaller than that of stocks and because the underlying demand for living space tends to be revised very gradually, the speed and magnitude of price rise and declines often observed in markets for securities are more difficult to create in markets for homes."

This perspective was shared five years before the national housing market crashed at a speed and magnitude never seen previously. Greenspan's tenure as chairman ended in the nick of time---in 2006---a year before the proverbial shit hit the fan. I'm not here to point fingers, but Greenspan promoted the generally accepted fallacy that residential housing prices would never go down on a national level. Given what we now know, it sounds almost laughable to believe in such a falsehood.

Today, the commonly held misbelief in real estate is that "everything will be fine as long as interest rates get back to 'normal'". In response to this point of view, I always ask, "How do you define normal"? If you're a 33-year-old banker, you never experienced the true cost of money until two years ago when interest rates climbed above 3 or 4%.

I was 11 years old when my family was preparing to move to the good side of town, and I clearly remember my father coming home with an FHA-approved loan at 11.75% interest. My mom was on the phone when he walked through the door, and upon hearing him come in, she put the receiver down and ran into his arms. He picked her up and swung her around the living room, Ward and June Cleaver style from the 1950s TV show "Leave It to Beaver". They were dancing with glee because anything under 12% was a home run back in the 1980s, and they couldn't believe their good fortune. The interest rate gods had smiled on them, and boom, off we went to the new house.

In the 90s, interest rates declined below double digits, and they've remained single digit since. After 2008, we remained on a slow and steady decline. There was a blip within the last 17 years when the Fed tried to raise rates, but everyone balked and moaned. Cheap money is too appealing, too sexy, and too easy for the markets and the politicians.

Historically, the average 30-year mortgage interest rate is often cited around 7%, and even after easing from its recent peak, we're still nowhere near the ultra-cheap-money era. People in my world bemoan the market slowdown, but they say, "Don't worry. Once interest rates go down, things will pick up again." Too many of us are holding onto the fallacy that low interest rates equal a healthy housing market.

Millions of Americans are trying to retain their wealth and protect their most valuable asset. For many, the only investment they've ever made is in their homes. It remains the best and safest store of savings. This long run of low interest rates has been wonderful for boosting asset values, be it property, paintings, or stock portfolios. Naturally, people want to see this continue. Especially Baby Boomers, who still control an outsized share of American housing wealth.

Economists and finance professionals know this is a numbers game, and fundamentals are not in place. When we believe that low interest rates are necessary to prop up the value of something, we've bought into the low-interest fallacy, a false sense of security.

Maintaining super-low interest rates indefinitely is unsustainable for any economy, but the USA has a double-edged issue in this regard. The United States still carries the largest sovereign debt load in the world, with gross national debt at roughly $38.9 trillion as of March 2026. Much of that debt is constantly rolling over and will need to be refinanced in this new, more normal rate environment. Historical examples, such as Argentina, demonstrate how excessive debt accumulation can lead to currency devaluation and economic instability. Serious economists now openly discuss whether today's inflationary hangover may eventually give way to a deflationary correction before the cycle is through. Prolonged zero interest rates typically create massive asset bubbles, while continuous borrowing and money printing, as seen in Argentina in the 1970s, eventually require an economic reckoning. The debt must be paid.

Greece's experience over the past 15 years serves as an example; after facing a severe debt crisis post-2008, the country underwent a decade of stringent austerity measures. This difficult period has led to a more stable economic situation, recently described as Greece's "spring." The concern for the United States is that without addressing current economic imbalances and having serious discussions about normalizing fiscal and monetary policies, we risk economic decline similar to what some European or South American countries have experienced. Worse yet, if the dollar loses its standing as the world's reserve currency, it's probably game over for US dominance.

People assume that if the banks continue to overpromise cheap money and face going under, the government will step in, like some financial fairy godmother, and bail us out, as it has numerous times in the past. The fact of the matter is that WE are the government bailout; we are the taxpayers, and if we're not paying the bill, our children will.

The Post-Covid Short-Term Rental Fallacy

Everyone's always looking for the next best thing, and Airbnb kickstarted the widespread adoption of an ever-increasingly popular, get-rich-quick investment strategy: short-term rentals. When it launched in the summer of 2008, Airbnb undoubtedly disrupted the traditional rental market as well as the hotel industry. The company's history from then until now is a fascinating one, but it hasn't been immune to market turbulence.

Before Covid, anyone with a garage, a basement, accessory dwelling unit (ADU), or an extra apartment made a ton of money by Airbnb-ing out their space. At first, Covid sent the short-term market segment reeling when everyone in the world was restricted from travel and required to stay home. During that time, restless humans were dying to go somewhere, anywhere. Most people worked remotely. They had the time, and they had an influx of free money from the government.

The Airbnb and VRBO market exploded because the only place people could travel was to a private home. Almost accidentally, people made a ton of money on their vacation properties because it became the easier way to travel and since most folks were also working remotely, that meant longer travel. The timing of the shutdown coincided with spring and summer; the kids were all in Zoom school or on break, and people were antsy for a change of scenery, more space, and the simple sensation of movement. I refer to the Covid shutdown as "Our Great Vacation," and Uncle Sam paid the bill. How many people do you know who just up and moved somewhere else for six months at the height of the pandemic? Note I say Uncle Sam paid the bill in jest, we as taxpayers will bear the brunt.

In the years since, the short-term market has remained steadily in demand but nowhere near the height it reached in 2021. A short-term rental fallacy was created based on these huge returns that social media gurus were quoting from that short period of time when there wasn't a lake house, a beach cottage, or an RV to be found. People started to think, "Hey, maybe this is a good way for me to make money. Everyone is cashing in. Why shouldn't I get in the game, too?"

Driven by the perpetuation of the short-term rental fallacy and exacerbated by social media, YouTube, and TikTok in particular, everyone from 80-year-old grandmothers to my 19-year-old daughter's ex-boyfriend tried to capitalize on their own slice of the pie.

When you type "short-term rental" into YouTube, pages upon pages of non-ending videos will appear looking like infomercials. There seems to be no shortage of "experts" out there, charging $10,000 a pop, claiming to teach people how to buy real estate specifically for this purpose. It's almost like the business of promoting the short-term rental fallacy has eclipsed the business itself. Said another way, creating the impression of a valid business avenue has become the business. There is an entire subindustry of folks promising "Make a million dollars a year with Airbnb," "Airbnb Property Investing in 10 Easy Steps," and "So You Want to Be a Short-Term Rental Property Manager."

In the abundance of YouTube and TikTok videos promoting this fallacy, the emphasis is that you don't need to have a lot of money to get in on the scene. One ridiculous proposal is to go out and lease a house to Airbnb, which means you have no equity, no control, and no ownership of the property, which is not even a strategy: it's stupidity.

Another avenue, probably the more common avenue that several million investors have pursued, is to buy short-term rental properties with a DSCR loan (or a Debt Service Coverage Ratio loan), which is a loan equivalent to the spark that ignited the bomb of the Great Financial Crisis in 2007. These loans are no different from hard money loans; they are not based on borrower credit and are structured in a manner that is ripe for fraud. DSCR are also shorter-term loans than the average 30-year mortgage. The originators of these loans borrowed money at 0 -- 3% after the GFC and originated loans at 8 - 9%, which was considered a very high rate a few years ago (but which is only slightly higher than the real average). So, the value that was attributed to the DSCR loans two or three years ago has changed now that interest rates have risen.

Critically, a DSCR loan is primarily based on the property's rental income. Rent payments need to exceed 125% of the loan payment. At lower interest rates, borrowers could get a higher balance loan based on the same amount of income than they can today because it's based on the ratio of the income to the mortgage payment. As interest rates increase, the value of the mortgage decreases.

Consider a Salt Lake City property that generated $100,000 in annual Airbnb income during Covid. Based solely on this income, lenders offered DSCR loans up to $1 million, with payments around $75,000-$80,000 annually at 7.5-8% interest rates. After Covid, the short-term rental market shifted. While the property might still earn $100,000 annually, DSCR loan rates have jumped to about 12%. For those refinancing, annual payments on a million-dollar loan have surged to $120,000. This change has inverted the debt service coverage ratio from a healthy 1.25 to below 1.0, pushing many loans underwater from a cash flow perspective.

Since mid-2022 when interest rates started their rise, default rates on DSCR loans nearly quadrupled.

Now What?

As a society, we live in a state of constant denial about how the economic market should be. We've come to expect low interest rates on our homes and record-breaking growth in the stock exchange. We overlook the societal transformations that have occurred because of Covid, the perils of climate change, and its impact on the real estate market.

Our human tendency toward denial has created an untenable bubble of fallacies under which we operate. History will prove our folly in this regard, but for those who don't have the time, the desire, or the lifespan to wait it out, we need to break out of the collective malaise and embrace a more nuanced, reality-driven, and forward-thinking perspective.

The realities of today's market and the factors that influence it have been established, and it's clear a financial typhoon is gathering strength. Some of the questions that keep me awake at night are:

- How do we manage the turbulence and ride the waves?
- How do we seek shelter from the storm and find opportunity amidst the rubble of what's coming?
- How do we fortify our economy, our marketplace, our financial systems, and our real estate landscape for the next one hundred years and beyond?
- How do we maintain America's dominance as the major world economy? I'm not interested in being a superpower, rather in being an economic and moral leader.
- How do we help others while helping ourselves and bind together as a society and as businesspeople?

My goal is to find a path to continued success in real estate, which we know to be the most historically stable investment. There is only so much land, and if you believe in rising tides, there is slightly less of it each day. But you know I love a good storm, so stick with me through these shifting waters as we explore a myriad opportunities on the horizon. In the next section, we dissect each of the prevailing forces this book looks to tackle, providing a necessary buoy during rising tides.

CHAPTER 3

Forces Converging

"The only constant in life is change."
-HERACLITUS

Why This Time Is Different

In the fall of 2007, I sat in a conference room with a dozen other real estate investors and lenders, reviewing our portfolios and discussing market conditions. Everyone in that room was smart. Everyone had experience. Everyone understood real estate cycles. And yet, not one person—myself included—grasped the full magnitude of what was coming.

We saw the housing bubble. We knew subprime lending had gotten out of control. Some of us were already reducing our exposure. But what we failed to understand was how the housing market connected to the derivatives market, which connected to global banking, which connected to insurance companies, which connected to pension funds. We were watching individual dominoes without seeing the circle they formed. When the first one fell in 2008, we discovered they'd all been leaning on each other.

I share this not to excuse our blindness, but to illustrate a fundamental truth about complex systems: the greatest dangers don't announce themselves as singular, obvious threats. They emerge from the intersection of multiple vulnerabilities that seem manageable in isolation but become catastrophic in combination.

> *This book exists because we're at another convergence point—one that makes 2008 look simple by comparison.*

The question I'm asked most often these days is: "When will the next crisis hit?" It's the wrong question. The crisis isn't coming. It's already here. It's unfolding in slow motion across multiple systems simultaneously, and because it doesn't fit our mental model of what a "crisis" looks like—there will be no single Lehman Brothers moment, no obvious catalyst such as a stock market crash—we're making the same mistake we made in 2007. We're believing the payoffs of old mortgages with newer, riskier ones was good news, not a blinder.

This chapter is about understanding that circle. About seeing not just the individual forces reshaping our economic landscape, but how they interact, amplify, and accelerate each other. Because once you see the pattern, once you understand the mechanics of convergence, the path forward becomes clear—not easy, but clear.

Convergence Creates Nonlinear Risk

Ray Dalio taught me to think in principles—universal truths that help us navigate an ever-changing world. Here's a principle that will govern everything in this book:

> *When independent risk factors converge, they don't add—they multiply.*

This is nonlinear risk. It's the difference between facing three separate problems that each have a 10% chance of causing significant damage, versus facing three interconnected problems where the occurrence of one dramatically increases the probability and severity of the others.

Let me make this concrete with a simple example from the portfolios of many friends:

Imagine you own an office building in South Florida. In 2019, you faced three independent risks:

- **Market risk:** The possibility that property values might decline
- **Climate risk:** The possibility of hurricane damage
- **Financing risk:** The possibility that rates might rise before your loan matures.

Each risk was manageable. You had equity to weather a market downturn. You had insurance for hurricane damage. You had cash reserves for higher debt service. These were separate buckets of risk, and you'd planned for each one. Then COVID happened and the entire universe moved to Florida with suitcases full of cash, driving up property costs for locals while creating a temporary windfall for businesses and property owners looking at the paper value of their assets.

Since then, here's what has happened in Florida:

- Insurance companies have left or tripled premiums.
- Actual numbers of weather events have increased in number and scale.
- Rising rates have increased debt service at the same time insurance costs surge.
- Property taxes based on the value of real estate have increased.
- Lenders require higher insurance coverage to cover more valuable properties.

- New buyers are factoring in all the above, reducing demand and slowing market.
- State insurance programs are underfunded and at risk of insolvency.

Suddenly, your separate risks have become an interconnected crisis. The market risk, climate risk, and financing risk aren't just happening simultaneously—they're causing each other. The insurance crisis is driving market values down, which is making banks nervous, which is tightening lending standards, which is further reducing buyer demand, which is accelerating value decline, which is making insurance companies more nervous about exposure.

This is convergence. And it's not a hypothetical—it's happening right now across coastal markets, especially in Florida with its classically boom and bust real estate cycles.

> *When you see convergence forming, your risk assessment can't be linear. You can't simply add the probabilities together. You must multiply them.*

In 2008, we learned this lesson with housing, derivatives, and banking. The lesson we need to learn now is that we're facing a convergence far more complex: a 17-year debt cycle is ending, climate volatility is accelerating, banking safeguards have eroded, demographic patterns are shifting, and technology is disrupting everything from work to warfare. Each is significant on its own. Together, they create something unprecedented.

The Three Primary Forces

While dozens of factors are in play, three primary forces drive everything else. Think of them as the major weather systems that, when they collide, create the hurricane. Understanding each one is important. Understanding how they interact is essential.

Force #1: The Great Debt Reckoning

Let's start with what I call The Great Debt Reckoning—the end of the longest period of artificially cheap capital in modern history.

From 2008 to 2022, the Federal Reserve kept interest rates at or near zero. This wasn't normal. This wasn't "low rates." This was a 14-year experiment in essentially free money, followed by an attempt to normalize rates that has proven far more disruptive than anyone anticipated, much of it under the surface and not visible to the general public.

When money is cheap for a long time, behavior changes. Not just individual behavior—systemic behavior. The entire economy reorganizes itself around the assumption that capital will remain inexpensive.

Real estate developers built projects that only pencil at 3-4% cap rates. Private equity firms loaded companies with debt because the carrying costs were negligible. Governments financed themselves at rates that would have been considered fantasy just two decades prior. Homeowners stretched to buy properties they could only afford at 3% mortgage rates. The entire pricing structure of the economy shifted.

I watched this happen in real-time in my business. In 2012, I could buy non-performing loans at 30-40 cents on the dollar because banks needed to clear their balance sheets and buyers demanded high returns to compensate for risk. By 2019, that same paper was trading at 80-90 cents on the dollar. Not because the underlying properties had become less risky or the borrowers more creditworthy, but because cheap capital drove investors to accept lower returns. Sponsors were just playing a spread game, and that's the environment the average 35-year-old banker or private equity executive grew up in. When money costs nothing, everything becomes a reasonable investment.

Then rates reset.

The Federal Reserve, attempting to combat inflation, raised rates faster than at any point in modern history—from near-zero to over 5% in less than two years. And here's what people miss: it's not the current rate that matters most. It's the reset.

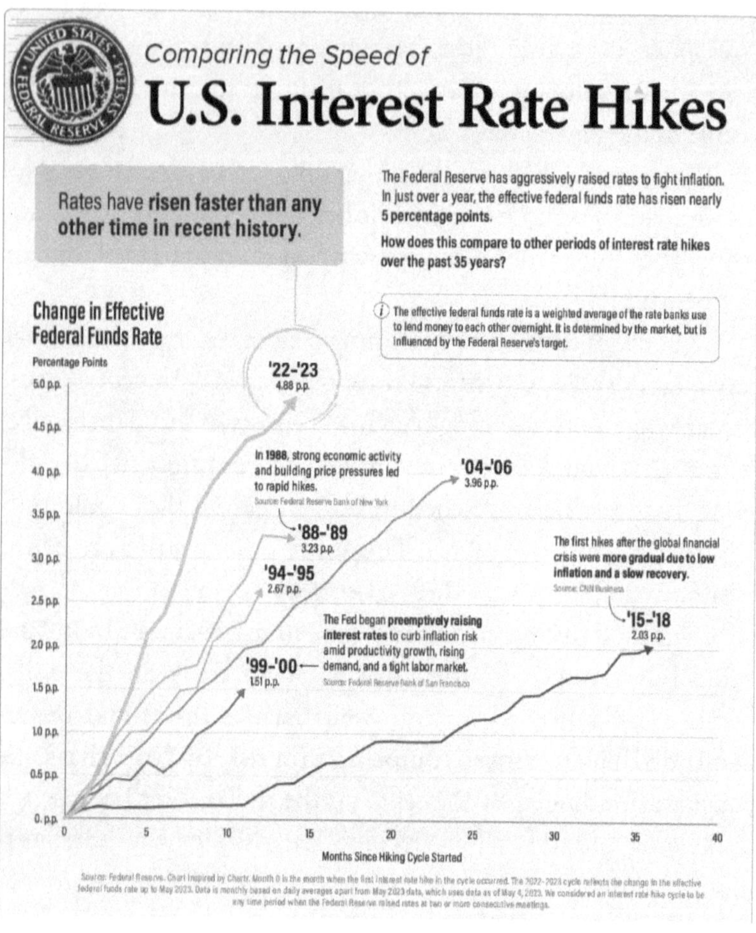

Trillions of dollars in debt were originated at 3-5% rates with terms of 3-7 years. Much of that debt is maturing right now, in 2026. Owners who could comfortably service a $10 million loan at 3.5%

suddenly face refinancing at 7-8%. On that loan, debt service just increased from $350,000 annually to $700,000-$800,000. That's not a marginal change. That's existential.

Can the property support it? In many cases, no. Rents haven't doubled. Operating costs have increased (insurance, utilities, labor). And the buyer who might have paid a premium price in 2021 is now demanding a discount in 2026.

This creates a cascade:

1. Property owners can't refinance at current rates and maintain positive cash flow
2. Owners try to sell but can't find buyers at yesterday's prices
3. Values decline, creating paper losses across portfolios
4. Banks will have to mark down the value of their collateral
5. Some owners default, forcing banks to take back properties in a declining market
6. Banks tighten lending standards, further reducing buyer demand
7. The cycle accelerates

We've seen this movie before—in the S&L crisis, in the Resolution Trust Corporation era, in the Great Financial Crisis. But here's what's different this time: the cheap money era lasted longer, the debt loads are higher, and the reset is happening simultaneously with two other major forces.

All cycles end. The longer the expansion, the more painful the contraction.

We're nearly eighteen years into an expansion fueled by the cheapest money in history. The contraction has begun. The only question is how severe it becomes—and that depends largely on how the other forces interact with it.

Force #2: Climate as a Financial Reality

The second force is one that many in finance still treat as a future concern or a political issue. This is a catastrophic miscalculation. Climate change is not an environmental abstraction or a problem for our grandchildren. It is a present-day financial reality that is already repricing trillions of dollars in assets. And we seem to be the only country in the world that makes climate a political matter, based on personal opinion.

Let me be clear about something: I don't care whether you believe in anthropogenic climate change. This is not about your political views on carbon policy. Those debates are irrelevant to the financial reality unfolding before us. The question isn't "Is climate change real?" The question to ask: "Are climate-related events increasing in actual frequency and severity, and what does that mean for asset values?"

The answer to the first part is unambiguous: yes. We can measure it. Insurance companies see it. Banks fear it. Reinsurance markets can't solve for it. And they're all responding to what they're measuring by repricing risk.

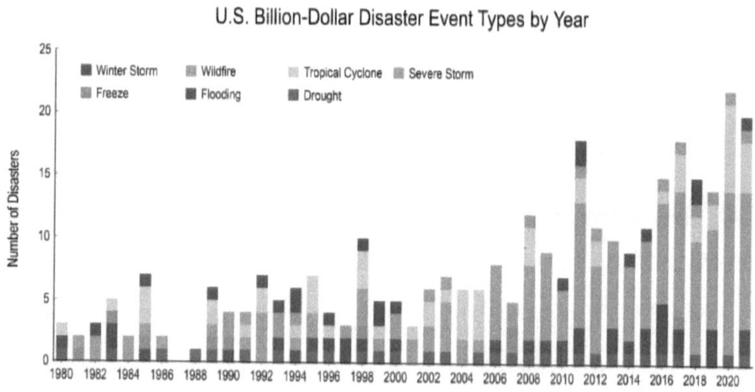

The chart above is the kind of measurement banks, insurance companies, and policy experts watch closely. NOAA's billion-dollar-disaster database was effectively frozen in 2025, but the series now being carried forward by Climate Central tells the same story: billion-dollar disasters are happening far more often than they did a generation ago. This pattern is the new normal.

Here's what that looks like on the ground:

Insurance Market Collapse

In Florida, where I've spent most of my career, we're witnessing the breakdown of a fundamental assumption that has underpinned property markets for generations: that insurance will be available at a reasonable cost.

Between 2020 and 2024, more than a dozen property insurance companies either failed or withdrew from the Florida market. Citizens Property Insurance Corporation, the state-run insurer of last resort, peaked at 1.42 million policies in October 2023 before falling back to roughly 336,000 by February 2026 as business moved back into the private market. That swing alone tells you how violently the market has been repricing risk. Citizens was supposed to be a temporary backstop, not the center of the storm.

The companies that remain are charging premiums that would have seemed absurd five years ago. Recent surveys put the average Florida homeowners policy around $5,800 annually for a $300,000 dwelling—and that's for properties that can get coverage at all. For waterfront properties, coastal condos, or older buildings, premiums of $10,000-$20,000 annually are becoming common. Some properties, especially commercial, simply cannot obtain coverage at any price.

This isn't a Florida problem—it's a preview. Louisiana, California, Texas, and other states are seeing similar dynamics. Insurers are pulling back from wildfire zones, flood plains, tornado regions, and hurricane corridors. Reinsurance costs—the insurance that insurance companies buy—have skyrocketed globally and major consolidation of these offshore firms creates an opacity that requires us to consider that their financial strength may be questionable.

Why does this matter beyond insurance costs?

Because insurance isn't optional—it's required. If you have a mortgage, your lender requires insurance. If you're in a condo association, your HOA requires it. If you're a commercial property owner, your investors and lenders require it. When insurance becomes unavailable or unaffordable, the entire financing mechanism is affected.

Banks can't lend on properties they can't insure. Buyers can't obtain mortgages. Property values decline not because the physical structure has deteriorated, but because the risk can no longer be adequately priced or transferred.

The Migration Effect

The second climate-related force is less dramatic but equally significant: shifting habitability patterns and population demographics.

Phoenix is experiencing more days per year over 110°F. Parts of the Southwest are facing "long-term drought" that may be the new normal. Coastal erosion is accelerating. Wildfire seasons are extending. Heat waves are lasting longer and reaching higher temperatures.

These aren't apocalyptic predictions—they're current measurements. And they're changing where people can comfortably live and work.

We're already seeing the beginning of climate migration. It's not refugees fleeing catastrophe—it's middle-class families making rational decisions about where to buy their next home. They're factoring in insurance costs, heat stress, water availability, and disaster risk. They're reconsidering that beachfront condo or that mountain retreat in a wildfire zone.

This creates a gradual but profound repricing of geography itself. Properties that were premium five years ago are becoming harder to sell. Not because they've changed, but because the risk profile has changed and demand disappears. In the vein of history rhyming, we've seen this pattern in the USA less than a hundred years ago. The Dust Bowl period of the 1930s brought drought and devastated farming, causing millions to migrate and deepening the Great Depression. From 1890 to 1920, St Louis was the fourth largest city in the USA at around 500,000 residents. Today it ranks 76 in population and wealth compared to the rest of America. Climate and demos played a role. And those citizens less able to move are left in dying towns, suffering the greatest.

The Infrastructure Mismatch

Third, we're discovering that our infrastructure—physical and financial—was designed for a climate that no longer exists.

Drainage systems in Miami were engineered for rain patterns of the 1970s. Electrical grids in Texas were built for peak loads that a good freeze can overload. Building codes in most of the country don't account for the wind speeds or flood levels we're now experiencing.

Updating this infrastructure requires capital—billions, perhaps trillions of dollars. That capital must come from somewhere. It may come from owners through assessments. It can come from municipalities through bonds that taxpayers will service. It comes from insurance companies through higher premiums. It comes from everyone.

Here's the convergence point: Climate isn't repricing individual properties—it's repricing entire regions simultaneously, at the exact moment when those properties need to refinance the debt they took on during the cheap money era.

A condo investor in Fort Lauderdale who bought in 2021 at a 5% cap rate with a 3.5% mortgage now faces:

- A refinance at 7-8%
- Insurance costs that have doubled or tripled
- Special assessments for seawall repairs or structural recertifications
- A resale buyer pool that's smaller and more risk-averse
- Banks that are requiring larger down payments and higher reserves for coastal properties, especially condos that are aged, some are not financeable.

Each shock alone is survivable. Stacked together, the math breaks.

Climate change isn't an environmental issue that happens to have financial implications. It's a financial issue that happens to have environmental causes.

Force #3: The Invisible Deregulation

The third force is the least visible but potentially most consequential: the quiet dismantling of safeguards that were created specifically to prevent the kind of systemic failures we experienced in 2008.

This isn't a political statement—it's a regulatory reality. After the Great Financial Crisis, significant reforms were enacted: Dodd-Frank, the Volcker Rule, enhanced capital requirements, stress testing, the creation of the Consumer Financial Protection Bureau. These weren't perfect solutions, but they represented an attempt to address the specific failures that led to 2008.

Gradually and systematically, these safeguards are being weakened or eliminated. Inside banks, special credit divisions once established to supervise risk and pre-empt loan defaults, were called Special Assets Groups. We will spend more time in a later chapter discussing SAG divisions, but what's important to know now is that banks have quietly done away with these divisions and an entire generation of bankers have little to no experience with workouts and risk pricing.

In 2018, the threshold for banks subject to enhanced supervision was raised from $50 billion in assets to $250 billion. Dozens of regional banks—including Silicon Valley Bank, which would go on to fail spectacularly in 2023—were freed from the stricter oversight and stress testing requirements. That obviously didn't turn out well for SVB.

The Volcker Rule, which restricted banks from making certain speculative investments, was diluted through a series of technical revisions that restored much of the proprietary trading it was designed to limit. Capital reserve requirements were loosened. Stress test frequency was reduced. Reporting requirements were simplified.

Why does this matter?

Because banks are not like other businesses. When a restaurant fails, it's a local tragedy for the owner and employees. When a bank fails, it can trigger a systemic cascade. We've understood this since the Great Depression, which is why banking has always been more heavily regulated than other industries.

The specific problem we face now is what I call "distributed fragility". In 2008, the risk was concentrated in a handful of "too big to fail" institutions. When they got in trouble, the government had to bail them out or their failure would have triggered a global collapse.

Today, the risk is more distributed. Hundreds of regional and community banks hold significant concentrations of commercial real estate debt—the very debt that's about to refinance at rates that may not be sustainable. These banks aren't systemically important individually. But collectively, they are.

If five or 10 or 20 regional banks simultaneously face losses from commercial real estate defaults, they could trigger a Lehman Brothers moment. They would create further constriction of credit availability and higher costs as banks pull back from lending, tighten standards, and work through problem assets.

This scenario is more dangerous than a single spectacular failure because it's harder to see and harder to address with emergency measures. There's no single institution to bail out, no clear moment when the government can step in. Instead, credit gradually becomes scarce, property values gradually decline, and the economy gradually contracts.

Here's the specific vulnerability: community and regional banks hold large concentrations of the roughly $5 trillion commercial mortgage market. About $875 billion of outstanding commercial mortgages are scheduled to mature in 2026 alone, and a heavy pipeline continues behind it into 2027 and 2028. Much of this paper was originated at rates and valuations that no longer reflect reality. The banks holding it are subject to less oversight, less stringent capital requirements, and less frequent stress testing than they were a decade ago. And the Federal Reserve gave banks several tools that allow credit managers to kick the can down the road, forestalling the inevitable need to work out thousands of dislocated loan situations.

At the same time, the specialized knowledge that banks once maintained in-house—the seasoned loan officers who understood real estate cycles, the workout specialists who could restructure troubled loans—has been outsourced, automated, or eliminated. When problems emerge, banks lack the internal expertise to work through them intelligently.

I see this firsthand in my business. I run a special assets group that banks and private equity hires when they need help with troubled loans. Twenty years ago, most banks had their own teams that did this work. Today, they've eliminated those departments to cut costs and defray attention from any potential credit issues inside a bank's loan portfolio. When trouble hits, banks will either need to rebuild this capability or outsource it.

This creates a bizarre situation where banks are simultaneously more vulnerable to commercial real estate losses (because of their loan concentrations and reduced oversight) and less capable of managing those losses (because they've eliminated the expertise needed to work through them).

In complex systems, removing safeguards doesn't reduce risk—it just makes risk invisible until it materializes.

Invisible is probably the best way to describe what we are seeing today in Private Equity. More and more public companies are being taken private, a move that many see as efforts to avoid public scrutiny. Private Equity has the least shackles of all industry and yet it controls a huge sector of the world's wealth, much of intertwined with the very same commercial banks that we've spoken about being fragile. If I had to predict a potential black swan in the near future, I'd say it will appear from Private Equity.

The Amplification Effect: Why 1+1+1 ≠ 3

Now the critical insight: these three forces don't simply coexist—they amplify each other.

This is what systems theorists call positive feedback loops, though there's nothing positive about them. It's the financial equivalent of a microphone feeding back through a speaker—the output becomes input, which becomes output again, each cycle louder than the last until the system fails.

Let me trace how this works: This is convergence. Each force makes the others worse. Each solution you might apply to one problem makes the other problems harder to solve.

Want to address the debt problem by lowering rates? You reinflate asset bubbles and encourage more risk-taking, making the eventual correction worse.

Want to address climate risk by requiring better building standards? You increase construction costs, making housing less affordable, at a time when people are already stretched by high rates and insurance costs.

Want to help banks by loosening capital requirements? You make the system more fragile precisely when it needs to be more resilient.

There are no easy answers because we're not dealing with a single problem—we're dealing with an interconnected system where every intervention has 2nd and 3rd order effects.

> *In a convergence scenario, addressing any single force in isolation often accelerates the crisis rather than preventing it.*

What History Tells Us About Convergence

We've faced convergence before, though not exactly like this. The closest historical parallel is the 1970s, when multiple crises hit simultaneously: oil shocks, stagflation, the breakdown of Bretton Woods, the Vietnam War's economic drain, and urban decay.

What made the 1970s different from the isolated crises of the 1930s, 1950s, or 1980s was that the traditional tools didn't work. You couldn't fight inflation with tight money without triggering recession. You couldn't stimulate the economy without making inflation worse. Energy policy, monetary policy, and fiscal policy were all pulling against each other.

Eventually, the system worked through it—but it took over a decade, required politically painful decisions (Volcker's interest rate shock), and fundamentally restructured our economy. Entire industries disappeared. Regions that had been prosperous declined. New centers of growth emerged. Mother Nature's cycles continue.

The resolution wasn't planned or managed—it was a painful evolution that left winners and losers scattered across the landscape.

Here's what history teaches us:

1. **Convergence crises last longer than single-factor crises.** When multiple systems are stressed simultaneously, you can't resolve any one of them without addressing the others. This makes solutions slow and politically difficult.

2. **The institutions that thrive are those that recognize the convergence early.** In the 1970s, companies that understood they were facing not just "high inflation", but a fundamental restructuring of global energy and trade patterns, were the ones that positioned themselves for the 1980s boom.

3. **The human cost is real and significant.** The 1970s saw unemployment, poverty, and social disruption that took a generation to fully recover from. People who lost their jobs when steel mills closed didn't just "retrain for new industries"—many never recovered their earning power. AI will accelerate this pattern. McKinsey estimates that by 2030, up to 30% of hours currently worked in the US could be automated—concentrated in the same administrative, clerical, and entry-level roles that historically served as on-ramps to the middle class.

4. **Government response is almost always behind the curve.** By the time policymakers recognized that traditional tools weren't working in the 1970s, the crisis was advanced. Emergency measures were implemented, but they often addressed yesterday's problems.

5. **New frameworks emerge from the wreckage.** The 1970s gave us new economic thinking—supply-side economics, monetarism, deregulation as a policy tool (for better and worse). The crisis forced innovation in how we thought about economic management.

We're at a similar moment now. The frameworks that have governed economic policy for the past 40 years—low inflation, steady growth, financialization, global supply chains—are breaking down simultaneously. Government volatility—regardless of which party is driving it—cannot bode well when mixed with climate volatility and financial markets that don't make sense.

> *Convergence crises are not problems to solve—they're transitions to navigate.*

The Choice Before Us

Let me be clear about why I've written this chapter, and why I'm asking you to consider these forces, and why convergence matters:

Because we still have a choice.

This isn't a prediction of inevitable catastrophe. It's a diagnosis of current conditions and an explanation of how systems interact under stress. The trajectory we're on leads to a significant economic disruption—but trajectories can be altered.

The difference between a manageable correction and a devastating crisis isn't the forces themselves—it's how we respond to them. Do we pretend they're not happening? Do we address each one in isolation while ignoring how they interact? Or do we take seriously the reality of convergence and start making decisions accordingly?

Here's what choosing to understand convergence means for you:

> **For investors and property owners:** Stop making decisions based on the assumption that yesterday's patterns will continue. Asset allocation, portfolio construction, risk management—all these need to account for convergence. The cap rates that worked in 2019 don't work in 2026 (the cap rates of the late teens never made fundamental sense). The financing and insurance structures that were standard need rethinking. The geographic concentrations that felt safe may need reduction.

This doesn't mean panic. It doesn't mean sell everything and hide in cash, although I do have many Florida investor colleagues dumping and diversifying out of the state. Ask different questions. Test your assumptions not against individual risks, but against combinations of risks. Build in flexibility. Maintain liquidity. Know your refinance dates and have alternative plans.

For bankers and lenders: Recognize that your portfolio concentrations may be more dangerous than your risk models suggest. Commercial real estate in coastal markets, highly leveraged properties refinancing in 2026-2028, and loans to borrowers who are already stressed by insurance costs or declining demand—these aren't separate categories of risk. They're overlapping vulnerabilities.

This doesn't mean stop lending. It means lend with awareness. Build in climate stress testing. Understand not just whether a borrower can service current debt, but whether they can service it when insurance doubles and a special assessment hits. Think about exposure not just by property type or geography, but by the intersection of debt maturity, climate vulnerability, and regulatory environment.

For policymakers and regulators: Stop treating these as separate problems requiring separate solutions. Climate policy, monetary policy, and financial regulation need to be coordinated. When the Fed raises rates to fight inflation, what does that do to property owners who are also facing insurance cost explosions? When regulators loosen bank oversight, how does that interact with banks' commercial real estate concentrations?

This doesn't mean more regulation for its own sake. It means smarter regulation that accounts for system-level interactions. It means being willing to act preemptively rather than waiting for failures to force action. And stop questioning whether climate change is real; insurers of every political persuasion price it into their models every day.

For all of us: Start asking better questions. When someone says, "the market is strong" or "we've learned from 2008" or "don't worry about climate—technology will solve it," push back. Ask: What are your underlying assumptions? What happens if multiple things go wrong simultaneously? What are the second-order effects? And does the person giving you advice really have the perspective of multiple market cycles? Mother Nature.

The greatest danger is the comfortable assumption that because we've weathered individual storms before, we'll weather this one too. We will, but at what cost.

The Work Ahead

This chapter has been about seeing the whole picture—understanding not just that we face challenges, but that we face interconnected challenges that amplify each other.

The rest of this book will explore our perspectives and each force in detail: how we got here, what the specific vulnerabilities are, and what it means for different sectors and stakeholders. We'll look at historical precedents, current data, and forward indicators.

But more importantly, we'll explore what adaptation looks like—not in the abstract, but in practical, implementable terms. How do you build a resilient portfolio in a convergence environment? How do you structure financing that can withstand multiple simultaneous shocks? How do we rebuild safeguards that account for modern complexity?

The storm is gathering. We can see it forming if we're willing to look.

The question isn't whether these forces will converge. The question is whether we can act in time to make a major impact.

In Chapter 1, we learned that all systems move in cycles. In Chapter 2, we hopefully opened your mind by recognizing fallacies. In this chapter, we've learned that when multiple cycles crest simultaneously, the impact isn't additive—it's multiplicative.

Next, we will examine what causes crises, how they've been dealt with in the past, and how technology creates its own set of concerns around climate change. Because the first step in navigating a storm is acknowledging that you're in one.

II.
ELEMENTS OF A CRISIS

CHAPTER 4

Ghosts of Crises Past

"The economy is the start and end of everything."
-DAVID CAMERON

The landscape of banking and finance has undergone several significant transformations since its inception, and every generation has a defining crisis. Perhaps you recall your parents bemoaning the economic crisis of 1957 that lasted until 1961? Or grandparents recounting the horrors of "The Big One" in '29 that sent the nation spiraling into poverty, foreclosures, unemployment, hunger, and suspended desperation for almost a decade. Most of us learned about the suffering caused by the Great Depression through John Steinbeck's, *The Grapes of Wrath*, required reading in my 8th grade class. Who can forget the Joads and their exodus from the Oklahoma Dust Bowl to California in search of work after being evicted from their farm? Mother Nature played a role there. What's interesting is that these same cycles have repeated in countries for decades, if not centuries. In the 1600s, tulips (yes, the flower that grows and dies) were used as a commodity, like gold, and it led to a massive bubble in financial markets that crashed miserably once everyone woke up from their tulip mania. Perhaps a 17th century version of the current crypto boom.

The Crash and Its Aftermath

After the stock market crash of 1929, it became apparent that Wall Street and the banking sector couldn't operate unchecked. They required some modicum of regulation and oversight to protect consumers. The crash is largely attributed to a speculative bubble in the stock market, fueled by easy credit issued from banks, and an excess of investor optimism (yes, I am talking a 100 years ago, although it sounds like modern day). Many people bought stocks on margin, which means using borrowed money. This practice inflated stock prices way beyond their true value. By 1929, stock prices reached unsustainable levels. When stocks started to decline, investors defaulted on their loans, the bubble burst, and many banks tanked. A wave of bank failures exacerbated this economic downturn when entire life savings were wiped out overnight with no FDIC insurance.

The Federal Reserve, created in 1913 by a handful of powerful moguls in response to earlier panics, faced its first real test during the Great Depression. Years of instability forced the government's hand. The Fed stepped in with monetary policy and liquidity for failing banks, but mistrust ran so deep that early efforts barely moved the needle. Eventually, buying government securities and lowering rates helped stabilize the sector.(It might very well be this move that causes people to associate low interest rates with economic stability, which is not technically always true. More on this later.)

The crash of 1929 triggered significant reforms that essentially led to the creation of our modern-day banking system. Specifically, the Banking Act of 1933---also known as the Glass-Steagall Act---implemented the FDIC (Federal Deposit Insurance Corporation), which guaranteed the deposits up to a certain amount. The Act also separated commercial banks (receiving deposits and issuing loans) from investment banking (securities trading). The separation was intended to reduce the risk associated with speculative investments and prevent conflicts of interest. Ironically, it was a 1999 GLB Act that reversed this restriction, a deregulation that played a major role in 2008 banking meltdowns. The SEC (Securities and Exchange Commission) was established to regulate stock trades, eliminate fraud, and enhance transparency.

Though not directly related to the banking sector, the New Deal initiated by President Franklin D. Roosevelt further boosted our deflated economy. When he took office in 1933, unemployment was at 25%, the banking system had collapsed, and many civilians couldn't afford to put food on their tables. New Deal programs included groundbreaking benefits such as unemployment insurance for those who recently lost their jobs, development of a Social Security system for retirees, and assistance for homeowners and farmers in danger of losing their property.

All told, the Great Depression lasted over a decade and affected every single person in the country in one way or another. Considered the longest and deepest downturn in United States history, it took a literal act of war to pull the nation up again. Hopefully we are not headed toward a similar fate. America's involvement in the Second World War created millions of desperately needed jobs and united a fractured populace toward a common goal. Shuttered factories sputtered back to life to ramp up wartime production efforts, and the collective standard of living vastly improved. After 1945, as countries around the world assessed their war wounds and faced shattered cities and economies, the U.S. enjoyed unprecedented economic and political power, a scenario Baby Boomers were born into.

Banking Busts

What happens when banks fail? Bank failure occurs when a bank becomes unable to meet its financial obligations and is unable to repay depositors and creditors. When a bank's assets, such as loans and investments, significantly decrease in value or become illiquid, while its liabilities, such as deposits and debts, remain unchanged, the imbalance in the bank's financial position can lead to insolvency and, ultimately, the closure of the bank.

Several factors can contribute to bank failures. These include poor management decisions, excessive risk-taking, economic downturns, asset bubbles, and inadequate risk management practices. Additionally, external factors such as economic cycles, regulatory changes, sudden shifts in market conditions, or unexpected shocks to the financial system contribute to the vulnerability of banks. The unspoken truth is that banks are very fragile business models. They rely heavily on leverage, and any significant financial albatross can wipe out any bank within hours. Trust in our banking system is simply faith.

Bank failures can have severe repercussions, not just loss of depositors' funds, but also disruptions in local economy, and broader systemic risks that can impact the stability of an entire financial system. And it's important to know that these are not confined to any particular type of bank or region of the country. Failures occur in both developed and developing economies and have affected large multinational banks as well as smaller local institutions.

People my age and older have witnessed two major banking crises in our lifetime: The Savings and Loan Crisis of the 1980s and The Great Financial Crisis of 2008. The S&L Crisis has been described as "a slow-moving financial disaster." At their inception in the mid-1800s, S&Ls were created as a means for homeownership and served as the launching point for residential mortgages.

S&Ls faced restrictions that other larger banks did not such as caps on interest rates, deposits, and loans, which hindered their ability to compete with other lenders, particularly when inflation kicked in and the economy slowed. That all changed with the stroke of President Ronald Reagan's pen in 1982, when he removed stringent regulation measures and incentivized S&L banks to take excessive risks through highly speculative commercial real estate investments with the hope of higher returns.

At the same time, interest rates rose sharply, causing S&Ls to be upside down on mortgage lending. The costs to fund a loan outweighed the income from the payment. Add in widespread moral failure, rampant fraud, embezzlement, executive self-dealing, poor risk management practices, and reckless lending, and it wasn't long before S&Ls had acquired a mountain of bad debt. By 1989, more than 1,000 S&Ls had gone under, and, according to Investopedia, it was "arguably the most catastrophic collapse in the banking industry since the Great Depression." The effect was an almost overnight devaluation of commercial real estate, especially in Texas, where many of the S&Ls were located. U.S. taxpayers picked up the tab for this catastrophe to the tune of $160 billion ($486 billion in today's numbers). We seem to have a history in this country of privatizing profits and socializing losses.

In response to the crisis, Congress established the RTC (Resolution Trust Corporation) to manage and resolve failed S&Ls. They also strengthened regulatory oversight and implemented stricter capital requirements and reporting standards. The FDIC and the Fed ramped up supervision of financial institutions, and hundreds of bank mergers led to the establishment of larger banks, supposedly better equipped to handle market volatility.

The second major banking crisis of my lifetime (so far) ---the GFC (Great Financial Crisis) of 2008--had a much greater impact on me personally and the residential real estate sector. Much like the S&L Crisis, the GFC was triggered in large part by deregulation: repeal of the Glass-Steagall Act in 1999 allowed commercial banks to engage in investment banking activities. Central to the more recent crisis was that banks and other financial institutions engaged in subprime mortgage lending during a housing market bubble caused by demand for new mortgages that Wall Street was packaging and selling to unknowing investors. Banks and private equity firms created complex financial instruments to maneuver around the governing bodies, who fell asleep and failed to adequately oversee corrupt practices.

Excessive risk taking, speculative investment practices, deregulation, and an inflated real estate market fueled both banking crises. Yet the scale and scope of the GFC was significantly greater, with blows felt painfully throughout the global financial markets.

Banks were going out of business daily, and residential mortgage loans were defaulting in double-digit numbers. The crisis was a public relations nightmare for the banks, whose unscrupulous practices were suddenly under scrutiny on the world stage. Every day, as millions of Americans faced foreclosures and evictions, the media depicted old grandmas being thrown out of their homes.

The housing market collapsed, unemployment grew, and again, the government had to step in to right the ship. Though experts, politicians, and pundits still argue about the exact cost of the bailout, MIT distinguished professor of finance, Deborah Lucas, argues the price tag was $500 billion, or 3.5 percent of the gross domestic product in 2009. Her number is based on a fair value approach, which considers the full range of future gains and losses and recognizes the cost of that risk. Regardless, and not for the first time, the U.S. taxpayers funded the bailout.

Free Money for Rent (aka the Discount Window)

The federal government tried to lessen the pain of the bailout by forcing the leaders of the country's top financial institutions to come up with a solution to fix their own mess and stabilize the panicked nation. The drama of these negotiations is beautifully captured in Andrew Sorkin's 2009 book, *Too Big to Fail*, which was made into a star-studded movie in 2011. Both the book and the movie detail the extensive role of the Federal Reserve and the Treasury department in the financial meltdown. They facilitated the acquisition of Bear Stearns by JP Morgan and resuscitated Fannie Mae and Freddie Mac (our predominant GSEs) by placing them in conservatorship and injecting them with cash. AIG, Citigroup, and Bank of America received hefty capital injections.

Critically, the Fed and the Treasury opened a lending arm of the government with their discount window, which is the rate the Fed charges banks to borrow money. Typically, this window is only available to federal or state-chartered banks and banks could expect a small "discount" or "spread," but after the GFC, the government cut that discount rate to zero. From 2008 until 2023, banks could borrow money from the U.S. taxpayer for nothing, charge their clients a lower-than-normal interest rate, and still make money.

Consider the following scenario. Let's say you're a mortgage lender. In 2009, your client, Jimmy, is struggling to make payments on the loan you signed with him back in 2006, when he was locked in at almost 7%. You and Jimmy have been working together for years, and you know he needs to stay in his house. Since you're able to get money from the Fed at 0%, you can call Jimmy up and say, "You know what? I know you're sweating the 7%. What about if we bump you down to 2% or 3%? You think you can make good on the payments at this lower rate?"

Jimmy, of course, is thrilled. It's not every day his banker calls to offer a discount, and this small percent decrease makes the difference between payment and non-payment. You draw up the new paperwork, Jimmy signs, and everyone is happy. It's a Win/Win.

The influx of free money from the government after the GFC allowed for an entire generation of modification workouts for distressed loans. It allowed lenders to cut the rates for delinquent borrowers in half if not more, and this practice became the norm across residential and commercial real estate. It allowed a lot of people to stay in their homes and hang onto their businesses. It kept the economy afloat, and management of real estate loan portfolios at state and federal banks underwent notable changes.

The Golden Age of Outsourcing Stress

Traditionally, the banks of the last hundred years were fairly self-contained. They managed everything in-house. Even in the early 2000s, there was an entire subset of bankers who were REO brokers, meaning Real Estate Owned. Those people managed the loans on properties owned by the banks, and banks directly serviced their own loans.

If someone missed a payment on their residential or commercial loan, they would receive a call from their local banker. And if multiple payments were missed, the individual would be rerouted to someone within the bank's Special Asset Group (SAG), which handled sub-performing, non-performing, and pre-foreclosure residential and commercial loans. Those individuals were highly attuned to their debt portfolios and were skilled at devising creative and workable solutions to mitigate loss.

In the lending world, it is commonly accepted that resolution efforts must be started within 90 days of non-payment; otherwise, it becomes exponentially more difficult to get out from under and the debt can snowball quickly. Banks recognized the value of being able to talk to borrowers and help them stay afloat. Something is better than nothing, after all, and in many cases; those hard conversations were made easier because, in the past, bankers and borrowers had a personal connection.

The real significance of the SAG division, staffed by senior bank officers and credit risk analysts, was they understood all the options and tools available to borrowers so they could custom tailor loan modifications or other resolutions. To avoid foreclosure, SAG officers understood the nuances of forbearance, how to execute consent judgments, avoid losses on refinancing, technical defaults and much more. These divisions were created after the Great Depression and continued to function until the GFC. Some of the larger banks and lenders have maintained skeleton crews, but an entire generation of SAG banker has not been mentored since there was little interest inside banks in dealing with stress directly.

At the onset of the crisis, the banks were doing anything they could to remain solvent, get out of the glare of the media spotlight, and offload the liability they'd accumulated en masse. After the GFC, banks dismantled their Special Assets Groups. Regulatory scrutiny and cost pressure drove them to fold loan workout functions into broader departments and outsource borrower communication to third-party servicers.

While all eyes were on residential real estate, most commercial loan distress was easily managed by bankers able to offer extend-and-pretend measures and lower rate bailout loans available during a declining interest rate environment.

The skeletal crew left manning the SAGs became accustomed to using an easy, unusual, and highly unsophisticated tool: free money from the government. The byproduct of this scenario is an entire generation of bankers and private equity professionals who don't know how to operate within the traditional rules of finance. The younger crop of bankers and managers at places like Blackstone, Black Rock, or Goldman must figure out how to make money in a system they have never been exposed to---a system with capital costs. This is the context through which half of today's banks are struggling. They've outsourced their talent and intellectual capital in exchange for free capital. And they've existed for almost two decades utilizing outside groups for primarily residential loans.

Fast-forward to the present day, and the banking landscape is once again undergoing upheaval. With interest rates on the rise and memories of the GFC fresh for older bankers but non-existent for the new generation, regulatory agencies such as the Office of Comptroller of the Currency (OCC) and the Federal Deposit Insurance Corporation (FDIC) are tightening their oversight of banks. This increased scrutiny stems from a desire to ensure financial stability, mitigate systemic risks, and protect the interests of depositors and investors. It also derives from a known fact that when interest rates rise, some sponsors will not manage it well and many deals will no longer pencil.

The Fed's intention behind raising interest rates is to starve liquidity and to try to bring normalcy to the market. What it's done instead is create a scenario where banks and lenders don't have an appropriate outlet for newly non-performing loans, which are on the rise in the commercial sector. So now banks are forced to attempt workouts internally for the first time since the GFC.

Commercial office buildings in major metropolitan cities face a double whammy because of the paradigm shift created by COVID. Several factors are creating instability and uncertainty in the commercial real estate market with the sharp rise of interest rates from zero to normal being only one factor. It's important to note that while banks outsourced their residential loan portfolios, most banks kept commercial loans on their portfolio, considering them as more stable investments. That stability fractured with the sharp rise of interest rates. Here are a few examples of the headwinds commercial real estate faces:

1. Interest Rates: Many loan officers, asset managers, and bankers are too young to know what a normal interest rate environment feels like and how to navigate that cost of capital.

2. Climate Change: Rising insurance costs are already having an adverse effect on commercial property prices in high-risk zones prone to hurricane, fire, flood, and tornado. Banks need to reassess seasoned mortgage portfolios to lessen liability by reducing exposure in these areas.

3. CBD Metro Office: Once considered the darling loan asset for bank portfolios due to their safety and security, downtown office sponsors now face huge vacancies, and many will default.

4. NYC Rent Control: In 2019, a new law stripped speculators' ability to convert rent-controlled and rent-stabilized buildings in New York and further limited existing operators' ability to increase revenue. Faced with rising costs and greater housing authority enforcement, many will default.

5. Multi-Family Dislocation: The fallacy that low-rise apartment complexes in middle America will price at sub 5% CAP is quickly disappearing and as maturities happen, MFR sponsors will default.

6. Geopolitical Events: The rise of tensions in the Middle East and Eastern Europe combined with concerns over a direct conflict with China or Russia, should be hedged. Chinese banks own the largest concentration of commer-

cial and residential mortgage loans outside the United States. The US is stoking fires with allies as well.

7. US Political Unrest: A rise in political unrest as well as continual mass casualty events is causing a shift in retail demographics as well as adversely affecting downtown metros, especially in cities where less enforcement exists, and crime is rising. Banks can address these risks now.

The absence of specialized units dedicated to managing distressed assets becomes a glaring deficiency. Without the expertise and focus of dedicated, creative teams made up of personable, problem solvers, banks will struggle to effectively identify and address emerging risks within their existing loan portfolios.

SAGs are a necessary workout group in the modern banking world. There is a false assumption that the world of debt negotiation is always contentious, which is simply not the case if the right people are in place. Seasoned professionals have the knowledge and the expertise to sit down with borrowers and have the hard conversation, to help them understand their options, and to guide them toward the best possible outcome for both parties. A lack of action in this arena can leave a bank vulnerable to maturity mismatches, loan losses, sharp increases in defaults, eroding investor confidence, and could further undermine the stability of our financial system, if this problem becomes systemic.

As the market tides shift, with rising interest rates and transformative forces reshaping the once-stalwart office-building sector, banks are exposed to an influx of defaults, distressed assets, and the urgent need to revive the specialized expertise of SAGs. Recognizing the need for enhanced oversight, banks must explore alternative approaches to managing their commercial loan portfolios beyond the role of the special servicer. One promising solution lies in engaging third-party entities such as trustees, consultants, private firms, or other banks to provide independent analysis and oversight. By outsourcing these functions to external specialists, a bank can benefit from objective evaluations, specialized expertise, and access to best practices unvarnished by internal motivations or politics. An external perspective can help banks to identify blind spots, challenge existing assumptions, and make more informed decisions.

CHAPTER 5

The Climate-Real Estate Nexus

"What is the use of a house if you haven't got a tolerable planet to put it upon?"

—HENRY DAVID THOREAU

When the Water Rises

I can tell you exactly when I stopped thinking of climate change as an abstract environmental issue and started seeing it as a concrete financial reality. It was 2002, and I had just moved back to South Florida after a decade away pursuing other dreams. I drove to one of my old fishing spots along the Intracoastal Waterway—a seawall where my friends and I used to sit like pelicans, dangling our lines for tarpon and mullet.

The seawall was still there. But something fundamental had changed.

As a kid in the 1980s, even at high tide, there was always a good three or four feet between the top of the seawall and the waterline. We'd sit on the edge with our feet swinging above the water, watching the tides rise and fall with the predictability of a metronome. That gap—that reliable buffer of air and space—was just part of the landscape, as constant as the Florida sunshine.

When I returned in 2002, the water was lapping at the top of that same seawall at high tide. In just over a decade, sea levels had risen over a foot in actual rise—and combined with erosion, settling, and shifting tidal patterns, the effective waterline had climbed dramatically. A few waterfront properties where we'd played as kids—backyards where we'd caught lizards and launched bottle rockets—were simply gone, reclaimed by the sea.

I remember standing there, watching the water, thinking about all the properties I was about to start financing and investing in. And I realized: this wasn't tomorrow's problem. This was already happening. The water was already rising. And almost nobody in the real estate industry was talking about it.

That moment fundamentally changed how I think about risk, value, and the future of property markets. Because here's the thing about rising water: it doesn't matter whether you believe in the science behind why it's rising. It doesn't matter whether you think it's natural cycles or human activity. The water doesn't care about your politics. It just keeps rising, one inch at a time, until one day your property is underwater—literally and financially.

Markets Price Reality, Eventually

Here's a reality that took me years to fully internalize:

> *Climate change is not an environmental issue that happens to affect real estate. It is a real estate issue that happens to have environmental causes.*

This distinction matters because it shifts how we think about risk. Environmental issues can feel abstract, distant, political. Real estate issues are immediate, quantifiable, and deeply personal. When your insurance company cancels your policy or triples your premium, that's not an environmental abstraction—that's a financial emergency.

When the bank won't refinance your coastal property at any interest rate because they can't get adequate insurance coverage on the collateral, that's not climate science—that's a credit crisis.

When the buyers who might have paid $2 million for your beachfront condo in 2019 are now offering $1.4 million in 2025 because they've factored in the insurance costs, flood risk, and special assessments, that's not politics—that's the free market re-pricing risk based on observable reality.

Mother Nature always prices to reality eventually. Sometimes it's slow. Occasionally it overshoots. But eventually, the price reflects what is happening on the ground—or, in this case, what's happening to the ground as waters rise, fires burn, and storms intensify.

Here's what's measured and documented:

According to the National Oceanic and Atmospheric Administration (NOAA), the United States experienced 28 weather and climate disasters in 2023, each causing damages exceeding $1 billion. That's more than double the annual average from 1980-2022. During the 1980s, we averaged 3.3 such events per year. Since 2020, we've average 18.9 events per year. Perhaps our focus on covid distracted this truth.

This isn't a trend line. It's a hockey stick.

When the frequency and severity of catastrophic events increase, everything built on the assumption of historical stability becomes mispriced and dislocated.

And in real estate, almost everything is built on the assumption of historical stability.

The Frog in a Boiling Pot

There's an old metaphor about a frog in a pot of water. Put the frog in boiling water and it will jump out immediately. But put it in cool water and gradually raise the temperature, and the frog will sit there until it boils to death, never noticing the incremental change.

It's not actually true about frogs—they'll jump out as soon as the water gets uncomfortable. But it may be true about humans. And it is especially true about those making long-term financial decisions in slowly changing environments.

I watched this happen in real-time over the past two decades in Florida.

My childhood in Fort Lauderdale was idyllic. We lived paycheck to paycheck, but my parents believed that if you lived in Florida, you should live near the ocean. First, we settled east of I-95—the unofficial boundary between "near the water" and "inland." Later, when my parents became more financially stable, and we moved farther east, past the railroad tracks, just a mile from the beach.

In the 1970s and '80s, Fort Lauderdale was paradise for a kid. Less than a million people. Small-town feeling. No cell phones tracking your every move. I had complete freedom to bike everywhere—to the beach, to the pier, through the more than 300 canals that earned Fort Lauderdale the nickname "America's Venice."

Those canals and seawalls were my playground. We fished from them, played on them, watched the tides move through them. They were constants in my childhood landscape, as permanent and reliable as the sun rising over the Atlantic every morning.

Starting in the early 2000s, areas of Miami Beach and Bal Harbor began flooding during full moons and ordinary rain events—"sunny day flooding," they call it. Properties that had never flooded in living memory were suddenly getting water in their yards, their garages, their ground floors.

Residents built higher seawalls to keep the water out. It bought them time. But some of those properties—the ones where my friends and I hung out as kids—are gone now. Not damaged. Not diminished. Gone. The ocean reclaimed them.

And still, the water temperature in the pot keeps rising. Slowly. Incrementally. Not enough to make anyone jump. Until Hurricane Andrew hit in 1992.

When Incremental Becomes Catastrophic

Andrew was a Category 5 monster hurricane that devastated South Florida. My family evacuated inland—we watched it on TV from a friend's house in Plantation, praying our home would survive. We were lucky. Andrew turned south at the last minute, sparing us the worst of it while completely obliterating communities like Homestead and Florida City.

I remember volunteering in the aftermath, handing out water and food. I saw entire subdivisions reduced to matchsticks. Decades of construction, possessions, history—gone in hours.

At the time, Andrew felt like an anomaly. A once-in-a-generation event. The kind of storm that old-timers would reference for decades. "Remember Andrew?" we'd say, the way our grandparents said, "Remember the '35 Labor Day hurricane?"

But Andrew wasn't an anomaly. It was a preview.

Since Andrew in 1992, Florida has endured a relentless parade of Category 3, 4, and 5 hurricanes:

- Opal (Cat 4, 1995)
- Charley (Cat 4, 2004)
- Ivan (Cat 3, 2004)
- Wilma (Cat 3, 2005)
- Dennis (Cat 4, 2005)

- Katrina (Cat 5 at peak; Cat 1 at FL landfall, 2005)
- Irma (Cat 4, 2017)
- Michael (Cat 5, 2018)
- Ian (Cat 4, 2022)
- Idalia (Cat 3, 2023)

Each one cost billions of dollars in damage. Each one has had lasting effects on communities. And the frequency is statistically accelerating.

We now hear of "once-in-a-hundred-year events" happening multiple times per year. The Atlantic recently published a piece titled "*Miami is Entering a State of Unreality*," documenting how the number of Category 4 or greater hurricanes in the last 20 years has increased over 60% compared to each of the previous three quarter-centuries.

Rain events that meteorologists call "once-in-200-years" have become routine. Invest 90L dumped unprecedented rainfall on South Florida in 2023. The National Oceanic and Atmospheric Administration forecasts that South Florida will see almost a foot more of ocean rise by 2040. Sunny-day flooding has increased 400% since 1998, with a significant spike after 2006.

This is the water temperature rising in the pot. And we're still sitting in it, arguing about whether it's getting warmer. In fact, since Covid, there's been tremendous investment and relocation to South Florida. Major private equity firms and hedge funds have relocated to Miami or Palm Beach because that's where their billionaire founders want to live. Just goes to show even the successful, uber wealthy class, can play the frog.

It's Not Just Florida: The National Expansion of Climate Volatility

Climate volatility—and I prefer that term to "climate change" because it better captures what's occurring—isn't a coastal problem anymore. It's reshaping real estate risk across every region of the country in different but equally consequential ways.

The West: Fire and Water

In California, the wildfire situation has evolved from seasonal threat to existential crisis. The Tubbs Fire (2017), Camp and Woolsey Fires (2018), and August Complex Fire (2020) each set new records for devastation. The Woolsey Fire was particularly terrifying because it jumped the 12-lane 101 Freeway and the Pacific Coast Highway, racing to the ocean. Nearly 300,000 people evacuated. Over 1,600 structures destroyed. Three people dead.

And then came 2025. The fires in Pasadena and Pacific Palisades caused nearly a trillion dollars in devastation in just days. Entire beachfront communities disappeared. The Woolsey Fire was a warning—but only seven years later, Malibu watched history repeat itself, worse.

As one local official observed: "Fire has been a natural and necessary part of our local ecosystem long before the area was inhabited, so the threat of wildfires has always been a reality for Malibu. However, the size, duration, and severity of the Woolsey Fire were unprecedented, and the new normal of drought and extreme weather due to climate change has meant that we have to make plans and prepare in ways we did not consider in the past."

A recent analysis published in *Nature Ecology & Evolution* found that the frequency and magnitude of extreme wildfires globally have doubled in the past two decades. Critically, as nighttime temperatures rise, fire intensity remains strong around the clock—eliminating the traditional nighttime reprieve that fire-fighters counted on for decades.

One veteran firefighter told me: "Twenty years ago, rarely did we have 100,000-acre fires. Now, it's common every fire season."

Meanwhile, in Arizona and Nevada, water scarcity is no longer a distant concern—it's reshaping development patterns right now. In June 2023, Arizona's Department of Water Resources announced it would no longer certify adequate water supply for new developments in the Phoenix Active Management Area. This effectively halted development plans for over 100,000 housing units overnight.

Think about the real estate implications: Entitled land with secured water rights now commands premiums of 30-40% over non-entitled parcels. Water—not just location or schools or amenities—has become the primary determinant of developable land value in the Southwest.

The Midwest and Heartland: When Rivers Break Their Banks

Tornadoes used to be a problem confined to "Tornado Alley"—the rural windswept plains of Texas, Oklahoma, Nebraska, and Kansas. As Dorothy might say, we're not in Kansas anymore.

The alley has expanded to encompass roughly one-third of the entire country, reaching into Alabama, Mississippi, Tennessee, Georgia, Illinois, Indiana, and Ohio. What was once a regional phenomenon affecting sparsely populated farmland is now impacting densely populated urban areas where property values are exponentially higher.

A tornado ripping through downtown Dallas or Memphis causes vastly more economic damage than the same tornado crossing rural Nebraska. And we're seeing more of them, in more places, over longer seasons.

Flooding has followed a similar pattern of intensification and expansion. Rodney, Iowa—population 45—may never recover after floodwaters from the Little Sioux River breached levees, wiping homes off their foundations. Parts of Union County, South

Dakota experienced similar devastation. These smaller communities often lack the resources to rebuild, especially when "hundred-year floods" start happening every five or ten years.

According to NOAA data, the frequency of major flooding events along Iowa's rivers has increased 37% since 1990. This has expanded effective floodplains well beyond official FEMA designations, creating uncertainty in real estate markets. Properties outside official flood zones but affected by recent floods now sell at discounts of 8-12% compared to truly flood-safe properties, according to Iowa State University research.

The Financial Cascade: When Insurance Markets Break

Here's where climate volatility transitions from environmental concern to immediate financial crisis: the insurance market.

Insurance is the linchpin that holds the entire real estate financing system together. Without it, the system collapses. And across multiple regions, that's exactly what's beginning to happen.

The Great Insurance Retreat

We covered the insurance crisis in Chapter 3—the exodus of private carriers, Citizens peaking at 1.42 million policies, premiums doubling and tripling. But here's what the numbers don't capture: the human reality on the ground.

Some commercial properties in coastal Florida cannot obtain insurance at any price. Let me repeat that: at any price. What was designed as a backstop has become the market itself—and that pattern is spreading far beyond Florida.

The premium numbers from Chapter 3 tell only part of the story. What they don't convey is what it feels like to be a property owner who's done everything right and can't get a carrier to return their call.

The collapse isn't localized anymore.

California tells a similar story. Seven of the state's 12 largest insurers have restricted new business or non-renewed policies in wildfire-prone areas. State Farm—California's largest insurer—announced in 2023 that it would stop accepting new homeowner insurance applications in the entire state. Not just in high-risk areas. The entire state.

The mathematics behind these decisions is straightforward: When the probability of catastrophic loss exceeds what can be reasonably priced into premiums while maintaining profitability, insurers have two options—dramatically increase rates or exit the market. Increasingly, they're choosing the latter.

Why This Breaks Everything

The cascade I described in Chapter 3—banks can't lend, buyers can't get mortgages, values decline, defaults rise, credit tightens—isn't theoretical anymore. I'm watching it play out in real time:

A client called me last month—a retired schoolteacher who bought a duplex in Pompano Beach in 2020 as her retirement income. She did everything right: 30% down, conservative financing, strong tenants. Three years later, she's trapped. Her insurance carrier left Florida. The replacement policy costs more than her monthly mortgage payment. Her tenants are asking for rent concessions because their own costs are rising. And her loan matures in September. I'm hearing versions of this story weekly now:

- Refinance rates of 7-8%
- Insurance costs that have doubled or tripled (if they can get insurance at all)
- Potential special assessments for flood mitigation or seawall repairs
- A buyer pool that's smaller and more risk-averse

- Banks requiring larger down payments and higher reserves for coastal properties

Any one of these would be manageable. All of them together create an impossible equation.

The Reinsurance Problem

The crisis extends beyond individual insurance companies to the reinsurance market—the companies that insure insurance companies.

There are only a handful of reinsurance companies globally, mostly offshore conglomerates with very little oversight and opaque governance. When reinsurance costs spike—and they have—it ripples through the entire insurance ecosystem.

Reinsurers are looking at the same data we are. They see the frequency and severity of catastrophic events increasing. They're repricing risk accordingly. And that repricing gets passed down to insurance companies, which pass it down to property owners.

It's a snowball rolling downhill, gathering mass and speed.

The Convergence: Climate Meets the Debt Cycle

Now we reach the critical point—the intersection that transforms a challenging situation into a potential crisis.

The debt reckoning from Chapter 3 set the stage. Now watch what happens when that math collides with climate. What makes climate the accelerant is that it hits the same borrower from three directions at once.

Now layer in the climate factor:

The same properties facing refinancing at doubled rates are simultaneously experiencing:

- Insurance costs that have doubled or tripled

- Special assessments for climate adaptation (seawalls, drainage, elevation)
- Declining demand from buyers who are factoring in climate risk
- Tighter lending standards from banks that are nervous about climate exposure
- Reduced rents or increased vacancy as businesses and residents relocate

This is convergence. The debt cycle and the climate cycle are cresting simultaneously.

A property that penciled beautifully in 2021—low debt service, manageable insurance, strong demand—is underwater financially in 2026 even though it sits on dry land. The owner can't refinance at terms that allow positive cash flow. They can't sell at a price that pays off the existing loan. They're stuck.

Multiply that scenario across thousands of properties, hundreds of banks, and dozens of markets, and you start to see the systemic risk.

The Market is Already Responding: Climate Discounts Are Real

Some people still treat climate risk as speculative or political. The market disagrees. The market is already repricing assets based on observable climate risk, and the data is unambiguous.

A study by First Street Foundation found that properties in high-flood-risk areas across America's coastal regions have already experienced $15.8 billion in lost appreciation compared to equivalent properties with lower flood risk. This represents a "climate discount" that's becoming increasingly pronounced.

Research from UC Berkeley found that home values in high wildfire risk areas of California declined by 6.8% between 2009 and

2019 compared to similar homes in lower-risk areas. That translates to an average loss of $23,000 per home in high-risk zones.

In Miami-Dade County, research by Harvard University's Center for the Environment found that from 2013 to 2023, properties at lower elevations appreciated 28% less than similar properties at higher elevations. This "climate gentrification" is reshaping neighborhood dynamics—historically higher-elevation, lower-income areas like Little Haiti are experiencing rapid value increases as buyers seek climate safety.

Hampton Roads, Virginia experiences "sunny day flooding" up to 15 days per year, compared to 2-3 days annually in the early 2000s. Properties exposed to such flooding sell for 7.2% less than comparable unexposed properties. The total property value at risk from sea level rise in the region exceeds $19 billion by 2040 under moderate scenarios.

These aren't predictions. These are measured market outcomes happening right now.

The market is already pricing climate risk.

Regional Spotlights: Different Risks, Same Pattern

One of the challenges in understanding climate's impact on real estate is that it manifests differently across regions. But the underlying pattern is the same: increasing volatility creates financial risk, which the market eventually prices in.

Southeast: The Insurance Death Spiral

Florida and Louisiana are experiencing what economists call an "insurance death spiral." As premiums rise, lower-risk property owners opt out or relocate. This leaves insurers with an increasingly high-risk pool, necessitating even higher premiums or market exits. The cycle feeds on itself.

We've covered Citizens' growth from backstop to primary insurer. The real question is what happens when—not if—a major hurricane makes direct landfall on a densely populated area. The state's exposure dwarfs its reserves, and federal intervention would set a precedent every other vulnerable state would demand.

West Coast: Fire, Water, and Regulation

California faces a triple threat: wildfire risk, water scarcity, and insurance market collapse. These factors interact in destructive ways.

Properties in California's wildland-urban interface (WUI)—where development meets fire-prone vegetation—encompass 11.2 million homes. Between 2015 and 2023, homes in high wildfire risk zones appreciated 12% less than comparable homes in low-risk areas. This discount is accelerating as insurers withdraw.

Meanwhile, water constraints in Arizona and Nevada are creating sudden value shifts based on water rights—a factor that barely registered in real estate valuations a decade ago.

Midwest: Infrastructure Meets New Reality

The Midwest's challenge is that its infrastructure—drainage systems, levees, stormwater management—was designed for climate conditions that no longer exist. Updating this infrastructure requires capital that must come from somewhere: property owners through assessments, municipalities through bonds, taxpayers through increased costs.

In many smaller communities, the math simply doesn't work. The cost of adaptation exceeds the tax base, leading to managed retreat—the gradual abandonment of communities that can't afford to protect themselves.

How Climate Breaks Traditional Valuation

Before we get to solutions, we need to understand exactly how climate volatility undermines the fundamental methods we use to value real estate. This matters because real estate professionals, appraisers, lenders, and investors all rely on these valuation methods to make decisions—and all three methods are breaking down simultaneously.

The Cost Replacement Method estimates property value based on the cost to replace or reproduce a structure. You calculate construction costs at today's prices, subtract depreciation, and add land value. This method works reasonably well for newer properties in stable environments.

But climate volatility has made construction costs wildly unpredictable. Material costs spike after major disasters as demand surges. Building codes are changing to require more resilient construction, adding costs that didn't exist five years ago. And perhaps most critically, the method assumes you'd actually want to replace the structure in the same location—an assumption that no longer holds in high-risk climate zones.

Would you really rebuild a beachfront property in Miami at current elevation after the next major hurricane? Or would you elevate it, adding 30-40% to construction costs? And if everyone elevates, what happens to properties that don't? The Cost Replacement Method can't answer these questions because it's backward-looking in a forward-changing environment.

The Comparable Sales Method examines what similar properties nearby have sold for. This is the standard method in residential real estate—the "comps" that determine listing prices. In theory, it captures market sentiment about value.

In practice, it's highly susceptible to booms and busts, and it becomes nearly useless during transitions. What's a "comparable" property when insurance markets are fragmenting by neighborhood based on elevation or wildfire risk? A house three blocks away might have insurance that costs $3,000 annually while your house faces $12,000 because of a slight difference in elevation or distance from vegetation.

The Comparable Sales Method also creates dangerous feedback loops in declining markets. Each sale at a lower price becomes the new comp, driving the next sale lower, creating a downward spiral that overshoots the fundamental value.

The Income Capitalization Method values property based on the income it generates. Calculate net operating income (NOI) by subtracting expenses from rent, then divide by the cap rate to determine value. This is the standard approach for commercial and investment properties.

This method is the most resilient of the three because it's forward-looking and tied to fundamentals. But even it breaks down when insurance costs surge unpredictably or when climate events cause operational disruptions that reduce income.

A multifamily property in Fort Lauderdale might have had steady NOI for years. Then insurance goes from $40,000 annually to $120,000. That $80,000 increase comes straight out of NOI. If the property was valued at a 5% cap rate, that $80,000 NOI reduction translates to a $1.6 million reduction in value—even though nothing about the physical property changed.

> *Here's the critical insight: All three valuation methods rely on stability and predictability. Climate volatility destroys both.*

When I talk to appraisers and lenders, many still don't fully grasp this. They're using methods designed for stable environments in an increasingly unstable world. The valuations they're producing are increasingly disconnected from actual risk.

This is why I'm seeing such a divergence between "appraised value" and "market value" in climate-exposed properties. The appraisal might show $2 million based on comps from two years ago. But buyers won't pay it because they're factoring in forward-looking climate risk. The property sits on the market, the price drops, and eventually it sells for $1.6 million—creating a new comp that pulls down the next property.

The Path Forward: Adaptation and Innovation

Here's where I want to shift from diagnosis to prescription, from problem to opportunity. Because while the challenges are real and significant, human ingenuity and market forces are already creating solutions.

Crisis creates opportunity for those who adapt early and intelligently.

Throughout my career, I've seen that the biggest opportunities emerge during transitions—when the old model is breaking down and the new model hasn't fully formed. We're in that transition now for climate and real estate.

What Success Looks Like: Real-World Examples

Some developers and communities are pioneering approaches that demonstrate how real estate can adapt to climate realities while creating economic value.

Babcock Ranch (Florida): This master-planned community north of Fort Myers was built with climate resilience as a core principle from day one. All homes are constructed to withstand hurricane-force winds. Power and internet utilities are buried underground. The community is powered by its own 150-megawatt solar array with battery storage.

During Hurricane Ian in 2022—which devastated nearby communities—Babcock Ranch maintained power and suffered minimal damage. The result? Home values in the community have appreciated 35% since 2020, outperforming the broader Southwest Florida market.

This is what happens when you design for future conditions rather than past patterns. You don't just mitigate risk—you create premium value.

Hunter's Point South (Queens, New York): This 30-acre mixed-use development incorporates elevated building sites, integrated stormwater management, and a waterfront park designed to absorb storm surge. During Hurricane Sandy in 2012, the partially-completed development successfully mitigated flooding impacts while surrounding areas flooded catastrophically.

The project combines affordable housing (60% of 5,000 units) with climate resilience features, demonstrating that adaptation doesn't require luxury pricing.

The Wharf (Washington, DC): This $2.5 billion development along the Washington Channel incorporated sea level rise projections into its design, elevating critical infrastructure and creating berms and terraced landscapes to manage flood risks. Commercial spaces at The Wharf command rents 15% above the DC market average—a clear premium for resilience.

These projects share common elements:

- They use forward-looking climate projections, not historical data
- They integrate resilience into the core design, not as an afterthought
- They demonstrate that resilience features enhance rather than detract from economics
- They succeed in the market because they're aligned with reality

The Innovation Opportunity

I'm excited about the innovation that will emerge from this crisis. Throughout history, necessity has driven breakthrough innovations:

- The moon mission accelerated technology development across multiple fields
- Henry Ford's assembly line revolutionized manufacturing
- The 2008 crisis accelerated financial technology adoption

Climate adaptation will drive similar innovation in construction, materials, insurance products, financing structures, and risk assessment tools.

We're already seeing early examples:

- Parametric insurance products that pay out based on objective triggers (wind speed, rainfall) rather than traditional claims processes
- Resilience bonds that finance infrastructure improvements through expected savings
- AI-powered risk assessment tools that incorporate real-time climate data

- Building materials engineered for extreme weather
- Distributed energy systems that maintain power during grid failures

The companies and investors who recognize this transition early and position themselves to provide these solutions will generate significant returns. The ones who wait for perfect clarity will miss the opportunity.

Practical Strategies for Different Stakeholders

Let me get specific about what different actors should be doing right now.

For Property Owners and Investors:

1. **Develop climate due diligence protocols.** Don't rely on historical data. Use forward-looking climate projections for your expected hold period. Factor in insurance costs, potential regulations, and market demand shifts.

2. **Conduct portfolio-level stress testing.** Understand your concentration risks. If you own 10 properties, and 7 of them are in coastal Florida with insurance exposure, you don't have a diversified portfolio—you have a concentrated climate bet.

3. **Invest in building-level resilience.** The ROI calculation for resilience investments has fundamentally changed. Backup power, flood barriers, upgraded HVAC systems—these aren't nice-to-haves anymore. They're value protection.

4. **Know your refinancing dates.** If you have debt maturing in the next 2-3 years on a climate-exposed property, start planning now. Don't wait until 90 days before maturity to discover you can't get insurance or that the bank won't refinance.

For Developers:

1. **Design for 2050 conditions, not 2020 conditions.** Use climate projections for the expected life of the building—typically 50-70 years. Historical weather data is increasingly irrelevant.
2. **Prioritize operational resilience.** Beyond physical resilience to storms, focus on maintaining functionality during disruptions. Can the building maintain power? Internet? HVAC?
3. **Engage communities in resilience planning.** Individual building resilience has limits. Work with local governments and other stakeholders on area-wide solutions.

For Lenders and Financial Institutions:

1. **Recognize that commercial real estate concentration in climate-exposed markets is a systemic risk.** Your risk models probably underestimate this because they're based on historical loss rates that no longer apply.
2. **Require climate stress testing in underwriting.** Don't just ask whether a borrower can service current debt—ask whether they can service it when insurance doubles or a special assessment hits.
3. **Develop workout expertise.** When climate-related problems hit properties, you need specialized knowledge to work through them intelligently rather than just foreclosing and taking losses.

The Choice We Face

I started this chapter with a memory of standing at a seawall in 2002, watching water that shouldn't have been there. Twenty-three years later, that water is higher. The storms are stronger. The fires burn hotter and longer. The insurance markets are breaking.

These are facts, not opinions. Measurements, not predictions.

We face a choice about how to respond to these facts.

We can pretend they're not happening—continue making decisions based on historical patterns that no longer apply, hope that tomorrow looks like yesterday, and be surprised when it doesn't.

We can panic—sell everything in coastal markets, declare real estate a dying asset class, and run for the hills (though the hills have their own problems with fire and drought).

Or we can adapt—make clear-eyed assessments of actual risks, invest strategically in resilience, demand better information and products from our partners and service providers, and position ourselves to benefit from the transition.

I choose adaptation. I choose to embrace reality and deal with it.

Because here's the thing about frogs and boiling water: Real frogs do jump out when the water gets uncomfortable. It's only in the metaphor that they sit there and boil.

We're not helpless victims of climate volatility. We're market participants with the ability to assess risk, make decisions, and adapt our strategies. The water is rising—we can see it, we can measure it, we can price it. The question is whether we'll make different choices based on that reality.

The markets are already adjusting. Insurance companies are repricing risk. Buyers are factoring in climate exposure. Developers are building resilience. Regulators are updating standards.

The real risk isn't climate change itself—it's being the last one to adjust to the new reality. It's holding assets priced for yesterday's conditions while the market moves on. It's assuming that because the water rose slowly so far, it will always rise slowly.

In the next chapter, we'll examine the specific vulnerabilities in our banking system that make this transition especially dangerous—and what that means for anyone holding debt or expecting to refinance in the next few years.

But first, internalize this: Climate is not coming for real estate someday in the distant future. Climate is repricing real estate right now, today, in observable and measurable ways. The only question is whether you're paying attention.

The water is rising. The choice is yours.

CHAPTER 6

The Hidden Vulnerabilities in Banking and Private Credit

"If you don't read the newspaper, you're uninformed. If you read the newspaper, you're misinformed."

\- MARK TWAIN

I'm going to let you in on a little secret. Starting in the summer of 2020 and continuing until just October 1st 2025, if you decided you'd like to take a break from paying your home mortgage next month be it a Fannie Mae, Freddie Mac, or even a conventional loan from any private bank---all you had to do was ask. No joke: thousands of Americans have taken advantage of a 2020 GSE mandate to servicers that allows them to move past due balances to back of the payment schedule or even waive a few months without penalty or negative credit reporting. This servicing payment loophole has created a five-year false impression about true default rates in our residential real estate market.

All banking institutions are regulated by the federal government, and our Fed has made loan deferral or forbearance a standard practice. Deferral is a short-term solution that allows for a temporary suspension of payments without interest. Forbearance is a longer-term solution that allows for either a payment reduction or suspension for up to 12 months with lender approval. In general, banks want to provide borrowers with options versus having them walk out on the payment altogether. Banks also need their loan book to stay in accrual (performing) status so that they don't have to reserve that capital.

Debt lending and collection, frankly, is a bit broken right now since Covid. Fearing the end of the world, or from another perspective, a tidal wave of foreclosures, the Fed told loan servicers they couldn't evict tenants for two years. The government has continued to extend this edict by making servicers jump through a whole host of mitigation hoops. The rules and restrictions created during Covid still apply to over 75% of residential mortgage loans. And because the industry is so large, no one wants to break trend with what the government is doing. Even in the case of non-government-sponsored loans, banks are instructed, expected, and motivated to provide modifications under any terms that work for the borrowers as a stop-gap measure of kicking the default can down the road. And they have more tools, rights, and freedoms to act with a "something is better than nothing" mentality than ever before. There are reporting regulations that the government has quietly loosened since the pandemic, giving banks the ability to rewrite loan terms on their commercial loan portfolios as well. This, too, has created a five-year false impression about the true rate of delinquency in commercial real estate. The Fed says they had to provide these tools to bankers to prevent massive banks failures and the resulting systemic risk. That statement alone should be a blinking red light, five alarm fire, to watch this space.

The Case for Personalization

Due to the variety of loss mitigation tools available and the variance between individual circumstances, a one-size-fits-all approach to loan workouts is not viable. In the world of commercial real estate, trying to fit a square peg into a round hole is a recipe for disaster. Each loan must be examined on a case-by-case basis, and here's why.

I constantly meet with bankers from all over the country. One such banker ran a farmer's and merchant bank out West. Most of his clients are in the agricultural business. The immediate challenge he faced was trying to figure out why one of his clients had failed to meet expectations for his nut production operation. The client had already refinanced through three good markets, but he was still struggling financially. The lender wanted to come up with a viable solution, but he was unclear about how to do so.

Another banker I met recently was a 33-year-old kid based in the Carolinas. He was handed a portfolio of DSCR (debt service coverage ratio) loans, which are non-qualified, non-government-backed, non-insured loans that his bank had purchased. The originator claimed they were no problem, short-term debts. But soon after the purchase, a good portion of the loans started to default. This young banker was contacting each borrower individually and digging into what was going on with each one of them. Realize that this 30-something banker has never lived through a normalized interest rate environment.

A third case I recently looked at was a loan for the development of a large piece of waterfront property in Boston. The plan included a marina, office space, apartments, and retail. The lender considered it a very safe LTV (loan to value), so he issued a $9 million loan on an $18 million property. The only problem was the International Longshoreman's Association of Boston got involved to block the development. So, the $18 million land is no longer worth $18 million. The lender was trying to figure out how to get made whole.

As these three scenarios demonstrate, there are so many asset classes, and each property and borrower has their own unique set of challenges. There's no way to impose a blanket solution for all of them. They require individual scrutiny and personalized attention.

The Human Side of Lending

I certainly did not get into buying defaulted real estate debt so that I could enjoy the benefits of debt collection. As a matter of fact, I find debt collectors to be my least favorite profession of people. What turned me onto this business was the uniqueness of each case, the creativity that is necessary, and the power that I had to positively impact individual circumstances in people's lives. It hasn't come without its challenges. One such example is a gentleman I referred to in my first book *Win Win Revolution,* and we will call him Cookie.

Cookie was an Australian gentleman who emigrated to the United States in the '90s and built a little nest egg for himself as a roofer in Florida. Cookie put his entire life savings into the purchase of his dream home, a1,800-square-foot ranch house one block from the water in West Palm Beach. When 2008 happened, Cookie was already in default. He had to stop paying his mortgage in 2007 because an accident falling off a roof left him unable to work. Bank of America was no help, and Cookie spent several years dealing with debt collector after debt collector. By the time we purchased Cookie's loan in 2010 (at a significant discount to what he owed), he was fed up and ready to fight whatever bank came after him to foreclose.

Cookie didn't see me coming. He wouldn't speak to me or any of my staff or my loan servicers. He would come to the front door with a bat in his hand and threats not to come on his property. So, I asked the judge overseeing our foreclosure to force an in-person mediation and the court obliged. Walking into that mediation room, the mood was tense. It took me over an hour of talking about anything other than the debt, just to get Cookie's blood pressure down to a point where he was engaging in a productive conversation. It took several more hours to get a loan modification negotiated, mostly because Cookie thought there was some catch to the debt forgiveness I was offering him. There was no catch, and we often pass some of our savings through to borrowers, why wouldn't we? If it greases the wheels to resolution, it's worth every penny. And it creates win-wins. We save Cookie's dream house, put him into an equity position again, and I got Christmas cards from him for several years thereafter.

What are the benefits of being a good lender? Being in the business of buying loans can serve multiple purposes, whether it be generating new business by originating more loans, servicing customers so that they may avoid regulatory scrutiny on their own customer complaints or attempting to recalibrate a dissatisfied public with financial regulators.

As a leader in the management and revival of distressed loans and defaults, I, and others in my industry, are in a highly delicate position because we are meeting people when they are at the lowest point of their lives. They're facing what can feel like insurmountable obstacles, the stress and practicalities of which threaten to take them down financially. Who wants to deal with the bank calling and threatening eviction for non-payment? No one. Sometimes, I think of borrowers as scared animals that have been backed into a corner. If approached incorrectly, they're either going to lash out or, more commonly, shut down completely, neither of which is productive for either party.

Essentially, those in my industry operate in an environment of disagreement, and we buy other people's problems, be they a lender's lawsuit or individuals facing potential bankruptcy. Many lending practices have been influenced by customer satisfaction because customer attraction and retention are necessary for banks to stay in business.

In financial markets and commerce, the truest measure of our success is not just the numbers, how quickly we foreclose, or how few loans go into default, but also the long-term business relationships and personal connections we forge with our customers and cohorts. By providing individual attention to borrowers, we transform a transactional relationship into a partnership, which is a win-win for both parties.

A win-win mentality is the precise approach that guides all my business decisions. I am constantly on the lookout for opportunities where all boats can rise with the tide. Though I've been using this approach since I first started my career, it became a necessity post-GFC. The collateral damage was so widespread that human-to-human empathy became a core job requirement. As a purchaser of defaulted loans, I do not take other people's problems lightly or discount the scars that financial derailment can leave behind.

The average borrower who finds himself upside down is usually a normal purveyor of real estate. They simply want access to the American Dream of home ownership. Most of those who require a workout or a loan modification didn't do anything wrong or improper. They simply got caught up in a storm they couldn't control.

The art of individual, loan-by-loan analysis is imperative because it offers a much-needed human approach. Borrowers want to be presented with the most and best options for debt resolution. They want a lender who will treat them with dignity and respect, someone who empathizes with their unique situation, and someone who comes to the table with compassion and integrity. People, in general, yearn to be heard, understood, and valued.

By truly listening and responding to the borrower's specific needs, we are doing more than simply providing a service. We are cultivating loyalty and building a long-term partnership for a shared journey to financial stability and growth.

A banker who treats clients as ledger entries destroys relationships. A banker who takes the time to understand a borrower's situation—their vision, their constraints—builds loyalty that pays dividends across cycles.

The new way of doing things quickly through technology and decentralization is efficient, sure. Efficiency might be a good solution for a short-term numerical problem, but efficiency doesn't serve humanity. This is one of the main reasons people are so worried that AI is going to take over the planet. If asked, "How do I save the world?" the robots will provide an efficient, logical, financially sound response, "Kill all the humans who have destroyed it."

When we try to apply large-scale solutions to individual human problems, we are adapting an AI approach that is unsustainable, ineffective, and ultimately inhumane. There's a total disconnect between the problem and the solution. It's like asking a heart surgeon to fix your teeth.

Shifting Tides

Prior to 2008, if someone couldn't figure out how to refinance a lower mortgage rate or afford their payments, they became a debtor in possession of a property or, in other words, a failed borrower. In most cases, by the time they reached that point, they either had to hand over the keys to the castle or go to court. When the GFC hit, everyone knew someone who had to give their property back to the bank if they weren't that someone themselves.

The attitude toward foreclosures shifted dramatically after the Crisis, especially at the banks. Since 2008, there have been very few reasons for a borrower to fail, due in large part to the volume and variety of financial products available designed specifically to prevent foreclosures. And let's not forget about the widespread access to an abundance of cheap money that led to a major uptick in real estate values.

The next few years will unquestionably look different than the previous near-eighteen-year market upswing. We will see a return to a more "normal" cycle, very much in line with trends we saw after the Great Depression and every other economic historical mile marker. Society has largely been blind to the realities that are staring us in the face, such as the inevitable evolution of market cycles, the myriad demographic shifts as a result of technology and Covid, the rising cost of insurance, inflation, and climate change. These factors precipitate the inevitable shifting tides.

We know from experience that any large market reset affects everyone on some level. When a national macro problem is on the horizon, we must come together as a society to deal with it from an "all of us" perspective rather than a "it's not my problem" singular perspective. And the way to address it properly and completely is on a loan-by-loan basis.

In the end, the success of our endeavors hinges not on the grandeur of our institutions but on the strength of our relationships. Let us, therefore, commit ourselves to the genuine care of seeing each borrower and customer as a unique individual deserving our full attention and respect. We are not just here to build profitable enterprises. We are here to build long-lasting legacies of trust and excellence. I get it. I'm being a bit grandiose.

Why Cookie Matters More Than Code

I think about Cookie every time someone tells me that technology and scale will solve the distressed debt problem. Cookie didn't need a better algorithm. He needed a human being to sit across from him and listen. That's not a feel-good sentiment—it's a business reality. The assembly-line approach to loan servicing works fine when loans are performing. When they're not, it makes things worse.

Here's what actually happens when a struggling borrower picks up the phone. They get a call center rep reading from a script, offering three canned options, with zero authority to deviate. The rep doesn't know the property, doesn't know the market, doesn't know that the borrower's insurance just tripled or that the city is about to assess a seawall repair. Every troubled loan is its own little ecosystem—a unique tangle of property condition, market dynamics, borrower circumstances, and capital structure. You can't fix an ecosystem with a flowchart.

Any senior banker who's done real workout work knows this instinctively. Each loan is its own story, and the resolution has to fit that story, not a template someone in compliance designed for quarterly reporting.

Making It Work in the Real World

So how do you actually do this at scale? You need the right people—workout specialists who can carry 15 to 25 troubled loans at a time, not the 1000-plus ratios that performing loan servicers handle. You need flexible tools that let your people model scenarios and access data without being straitjacketed by rigid workflows. And most importantly, you need a culture that values the long game over the quarterly efficiency metric. That means leadership willing to measure success by how many borrowers stay in their properties and how much value gets preserved—not just how fast files get closed.

None of this is cheap, and none of it is easy. But it's a better choice than the alternative. The Midwest bank I mentioned earlier—the one with 400 non-performing loans and three people trying to manage them—ended up taking losses they could have avoided with a fraction of the investment in proper workout staffing. The math isn't complicated: personalized attention costs more per loan but saves multiples of that cost in avoided foreclosures and preserved value.

And this is only going to matter more. As climate risk makes every property's risk profile more unique, as markets fracture along lines that traditional classifications can't capture, and as the convergence forces I've described in this book create distress that doesn't fit any existing playbook—the case for human judgment, creativity, and individual attention only gets stronger.

Private Credit and the Blue Owl

It's not my style to title a chapter about vulnerabilities in banking and private credit and then leave you hanging without naming the pocket of the market I keep circling. I have been on record for some time predicting that the next major crack may come by way of private credit and private equity. As of early 2026, the IMF is still warning that the fast-growing private-credit market warrants closer scrutiny, and Stanford researchers have warned that the democratization of private equity could create a systemic-risk machine. Some large alternative-asset firms have already had to gate redemptions or explain sharp public-market volatility in vehicles tied to these strategies. Much of that ecosystem also touches banks and other non-bank financial intermediaries. The opacity alone should make us cautious.

The institutions that figure this out—that look for deals that make no sense and invest in people who can sit across from a Cookie to find a path forward—will be the ones that turn market disruptions into opportunities. The ones that keep running the machine will be the ones that end up feeding properties into a falling market, wondering why their recovery rates keep dropping. The gifts of Mother Nature.

CHAPTER 7

Technology's Dual Role in The Climate Crisis

"All models are wrong, but some are useful."
—GEORGE E. P. BOX

The Green Dashboard That Lied

I remember sitting in my office in Fort Lauderdale in late 2019, reviewing our commercial real estate portfolio on what our tech vendor proudly called their "next-generation risk management platform." The dashboard was beautiful—clean design, real-time data feeds, automated risk scores calculated by sophisticated algorithms trained on decades of lending history. Everything looked great. Green lights across the board. The algorithm's risk scores showed our coastal properties as "acceptable" to "low risk."

Then I did something old-fashioned: I got in my car and drove to one of these "low risk" properties—a mixed-use development three blocks from Fort Lauderdale beach that our dashboard showed as one of our strongest performers.

The building manager met me in the parking lot. She was frustrated, exhausted. "Bill, I don't know what to tell you anymore.

The insurance renewed last month at three times last year's cost. Three of our commercial tenants gave notice because their own insurers won't cover businesses this close to the water. The condo association across the street just hit owners with a $50,000 special assessment for seawall repairs. And I've got two prospective buyers who walked away after their insurance quotes came back."

I pulled out my phone, opened our fancy dashboard, looked at this property. Still green. Still "low risk." Still showing strong fundamentals based on historical performance patterns.

That's when I understood something crucial: our technology was optimized for yesterday's world, but we were living in tomorrow's crisis.

Technology didn't create the climate crisis by itself—but it sure as hell enabled the real estate bubble that's now colliding with it. And now, that same technology is making the collision happen faster and harder than it otherwise would have.

How Technology Built the House of Cards

Let's be honest about how we got here. The convergence of debt, climate, and banking vulnerabilities that I outlined in Chapter 3 wasn't inevitable—it was engineered. And technology was the primary engineering tool.

In my three decades in real estate finance, I've watched technology transform from a back-office function into the driving force behind how properties are valued, financed, and traded. Each innovation promised to make markets more efficient, more transparent, more rational. Instead, they often just made it easier to make bigger mistakes faster.

The Algorithmic Lending Era

Start with automated underwriting systems. When I began in this business in the early 2000s, underwriting a commercial loan meant sending someone to physically inspect the property, talk to the borrower face-to-face, understand the local market dynamics. It took time. It required judgment. It was expensive and inefficient.

Then came the algorithms.

By the mid-2000s, banks were using automated valuation models (AVMs) that could assess a property without anyone stepping foot inside. Digital underwriting platforms could process applications in days rather than weeks. Risk scoring algorithms trained on historical data could make credit decisions faster than any human loan officer.

This wasn't inherently bad. Automation democratized access to capital and reduced obvious biases. But it created a hidden vulnerability: the algorithms were trained on historical data that assumed climate stability, insurance availability, and interest rates that would remain low forever.

The technology was brilliant at detecting historical patterns of default—borrower credit scores, debt-to-income ratios, loan-to-value calculations. But it couldn't detect emergent systemic risks that had never appeared in the training data.

How do you train an algorithm to detect "insurance market collapse in previously stable regions" when that's never happened before at scale? You don't. The model marks it "low risk" because history says it's low risk. Right up until history breaks.

The Securitization Engine

Then there's securitization—the process of bundling loans into tradable securities. Technology made this not just possible but routine.

I watched this machine get built in real-time. Sophisticated models could slice and dice thousands of loans into tranches with computer-generated precision. Rating agencies used proprietary algorithms to assign credit ratings. Trading platforms made these securities liquid and global.

Again, not inherently bad. Securitization spreads risk and connects capital to opportunities. But it also creates distance between the loan originator and the ultimate risk-bearer. And that distance encourages carelessness.

When I'm lending my own money to a borrower I'll see again next month, I pay attention to details. When I'm originating loans to sell into a securitization pool that some pension fund in Norway will end up holding, the incentives change. The technology that enables this distance looks like efficiency—but it's actually what Nassim Taleb would call "hidden fragility."

The Dashboard Delusion

Finally, there's the seductive power of real-time data visualization. Modern property management platforms give owners and lenders the illusion of total transparency. You can see occupancy rates, rent rolls, maintenance costs, NOI calculations—all updating in real-time, all looking sophisticated and scientific.

But here's what those dashboards don't show you: the insurance broker who's quietly advising tenants to relocate before next hurricane season. City engineer concerned about the stormwater system capacity. A building inspector who noted foundation cracks during the last inspection. The insurance underwriter who's been directed to exit this market over the next 18 months.

Technology excels at quantifying the quantifiable. It fails at capturing the qualitative signals that often matter most in complex situations. And in a convergence crisis—where financial, climate, and regulatory factors interact in novel ways—the qualitative often overwhelms the quantitative.

I learned this lesson the hard way with that Fort Lauderdale property. The dashboard was truthfully reporting the data it could measure. But the data it could measure wasn't the data that mattered.

Technology as Convergence Accelerator

Here's what keeps me up at night: technology isn't just failing to warn us about the convergence—it's making the convergence happen faster and more violently.

Price Discovery in Real-Time

Twenty years ago, if your coastal property was losing value due to climate risk, it took time for the market to discover this. Comparable sales happened slowly. Information spread through word-of-mouth and local relationships. The repricing process was gradual, giving owners time to adapt.

Not anymore.

Today, platforms like Zillow, Redfin, and CoStar provide instant access to comparable sales data. Climate risk assessments from FirstStreet.org are publicly available and increasingly integrated into MLS listings. Insurance cost data is increasingly transparent. Flood maps update in real-time.

This transparency is supposed to be good—and in theory, it is. But in practice, it means that when a market starts repricing for climate risk, the repricing happens fast. Really fast.

I'm watching this in Florida right now. Properties in high-risk zones that maintained value through 2021 saw 10-15% discounts appear in 2022-2023. Not because the properties physically changed, but because information about insurance costs, climate risk, and regulatory changes became widely available simultaneously.

For individual property owners trying to sell before refinancing, this is catastrophic. The market reprices their asset while they're still carrying yesterday's debt at tomorrow's interest rate.

The Correlation Cascade

Technology also reveals correlations that were previously hidden. This sounds good until you realize what it means.

Banks used to think they had diversified portfolios because they had properties spread across different cities, different property types, different borrowers. Then sophisticated portfolio analytics revealed that many of these "diverse" holdings were actually correlated through climate risk exposure, insurance market dependencies, or common debt maturity dates.

I've seen banks suddenly realize that 40% of their commercial portfolio had the same risk profile they thought was spread across 5%. The technology that revealed this is the same technology that allows rating agencies, regulators, and equity analysts to see it too.

Once everyone can see the concentration risk, it stops being priced as diversification and starts being priced as concentration. The technology that made the risk visible also made it real.

The Algorithmic Exodus

Perhaps most concerning is how technology might accelerate capital flight from climate-vulnerable markets, although it's hardly happened that way in South Florida.

Institutional investors increasingly use algorithmic portfolio management systems. These systems don't have emotional attachments to places or communities. They have risk parameters and return targets.

As climate risk data becomes more sophisticated and widely available, these algorithms will identify vulnerable markets faster than human portfolio managers would. And they'll exit those positions without hesitation or sentiment.

I've had conversations with fund managers who tell me their risk systems are already flagging coastal markets for reduced allocation. Not because of any specific event—simply because the forward-looking climate models crossed internal thresholds.

When capital is algorithmic and footloose, and when climate risk data is real-time and precise, the exodus from vulnerable markets won't be gradual. It'll be sudden. And it'll be self-reinforcing—because once capital starts leaving, that becomes its own signal for more capital to leave.

Technology as Potential Solution

Now, I don't want you to think I'm anti-technology. I'm not. I use sophisticated tech tools in my business every day. Technology has enabled capabilities that can genuinely help us navigate this crisis.

But—and this is crucial—technology only helps when it's deployed with clear eyes about both its capabilities and limitations.

Building-Level Resilience Technology

Some of the most promising technology applications are at the building level—making individual properties more resilient to climate impacts.

I've worked with properties that have implemented:

- **Advanced hurricane protection:** Impact-resistant windows and doors, reinforced roof connections, backup power systems with automatic switchover. One property I advised in Miami Beach invested $300,000 in upgrades and saw their insurance premium drop from $48,000 to $28,000 annually. Payback period: 15 years on the insurance savings alone, but they also increased property value and reduced catastrophic loss risk.

- **Distributed energy systems:** Solar panels combined with battery storage. During Hurricane Ian, properties with these systems maintained power for days while the grid was down. This isn't just about sustainability—it's about operational continuity, which translates directly to tenant retention and property value.

- **Smart water management:** Advanced leak detection systems, automated shutoff valves, water pressure monitoring. One property we work with caught a pipe failure within minutes rather than hours, preventing $200,000 in water damage. Over time, these systems reduce insurance claims, which reduces premiums, which improves NOI.

- **Climate adaptation infrastructure:** Elevated mechanicals, flood-resistant materials, enhanced drainage. These aren't sexy tech plays, but they're grounded in physics and engineering. They work.

> *The key insight: technology is most effective when it's solving specific, concrete problems at the property level. Where it tends to fail is when we expect it to solve systemic problems that require institutional and behavioral change.*

Portfolio Risk Assessment Tools

At the portfolio level, technology can help identify concentrations and vulnerabilities faster than traditional methods.

My firm uses climate risk analytics platforms to stress-test our portfolio against various scenarios: Category 5 hurricane hitting Southeast Florida, insurance market complete collapse in Louisiana, 500-year flood events in Houston.

These tools don't predict the future—but they reveal which properties would be most exposed under various futures. That information drives capital allocation decisions, reserve requirements, insurance strategies.

The critical difference from the "dashboard delusion" I described earlier: these tools are being used to ask "what if" questions, not to declare "all clear." We're using technology to explore scenarios, not to certify safety.

Insurance Innovation

Technology is also enabling new insurance products that better match climate risk realities.

- **Parametric insurance** pays out automatically when specific triggers are met (wind speed over 130 mph, rainfall over 10 inches, flood depth over 3 feet) rather than requiring claims adjustment. This speeds recovery and reduces disputes.
- **Usage-based insurance** monitors actual conditions and adjusts pricing accordingly. Some insurers are offering

lower rates to buildings with smart monitoring systems that can prevent small problems from becoming big claims.

- **Peer-to-peer risk pools** use blockchain technology to create smaller, more transparent insurance collectives that align incentives better than traditional insurance.

I'm not saying these solve the insurance crisis—they don't. But they represent creative uses of technology to adapt to new realities rather than futilely trying to preserve old models.

Information Systems for Early Warning

Technology excels at monitoring and signaling when used appropriately.

Satellite imaging can detect coastal erosion, vegetation stress, infrastructure degradation before it's visible on the ground. IoT sensors can monitor building performance, detect anomalies, trigger maintenance before failures.

Weather forecasting has improved dramatically—we now get 5-7 days of reliable hurricane track predictions versus 2-3 days a generation ago. This matters enormously for property protection, evacuation decisions, supply chain management.

The key is using these systems for their actual purpose: early warning that enables human decision-making. Not as substitutes for judgment, but as tools to inform judgment.

The Limits of Technological Salvation

After spending considerable time on technology's potential contributions, I need to be clear about something: **technology will not save us from the convergence crisis.**

I've seen too many people place excessive faith in technological solutions to problems that are fundamentally institutional, behavioral, and political.

The Efficiency Paradox

Take energy efficiency technology—LED lights, efficient HVAC systems, better insulation. These are good things. But there's a paradox: as buildings become more energy-efficient, they often become larger, more numerous, or more intensively used.

This is Jevons Paradox, which economists have understood since the 1860s: efficiency improvements often increase rather than decrease total resource consumption because they lower the effective cost of consumption.

I see this in real estate constantly. Energy-efficient building technology makes it economically viable to develop in more remote locations, increase square footage per capita, maintain more extreme indoor temperatures. The efficiency enables expansion that often negates the efficiency gains.

Technology doesn't solve behavioral and systemic problems. It just makes those problems manifest differently.

The Problem-Shifting Trap

Technology often moves problems rather than solving them.

Electric vehicles are celebrated as climate solutions—and they're better than gas vehicles in many ways. But the mining required for batteries creates environmental problems. The charging infrastructure requires massive electricity generation. The disposal creates waste challenges.

I'm not arguing against EVs—I'm arguing against the magical thinking that says technology makes problems disappear rather than transform them.

In real estate, I see this with "green building" technology. Buildings certified LEED Platinum often have enormous, embodied carbon in their materials and construction. A green building placed in an auto-dependent suburb might generate more emissions than a conventional building in a walkable urban neighborhood.

Technology is a tool. Tools can be used well or poorly. Using tools well requires understanding systems, not just components. And investment in new technologies can certainly provide for new jobs in the future.

The Implementation Gap

Finally, there's the brutal reality of implementation gaps. We often have the technology to do better—but lack the institutional structures, economic incentives, and political will to deploy it at scale.

Solar and wind are now cheaper than fossil fuels in most markets. We have the technology for a clean energy transition. What we lack is the infrastructure, the storage capacity, the regulatory frameworks, and the financial models to make it happen at the required speed.

In my field, we have the technology to assess climate risk, adapt buildings, restructure portfolios. What we lack is banks willing to abandon practices that have worked for decades, regulators who understand these novel risks, insurance markets willing to operate in transformed conditions.

Technology enables. It doesn't compel. And in a world where the enabling technology is racing ahead of institutional adaptation, the gaps between what's possible and what's actual create their own risks.

Practical Wisdom for Navigating Technology's Role

So, what should you do with this understanding?

1. Use technology as telescope, not oracle

Technology excels at revealing patterns, providing data, expanding our field of view. It's terrible at certainty, prediction, and replacing judgment.

Deploy technology to see further and more clearly. Don't deploy it hoping it will tell you what to do. That's still your job.

2. Default to low-tech resilience

When evaluating resilience investments, favor physical, passive solutions over complex technological ones.

A property elevated above flood level doesn't depend on sensors, algorithms, or network connectivity. Impact-resistant windows don't need software updates. Backup generators are technology, but they're simple, testable technology.

The more complex the technology, the more ways it can fail. In crisis scenarios, simple and robust usually beats complex and optimal.

3. Maintain redundancy in critical systems

Don't let technology create single points of failure.

Keep paper copies of critical documents. Maintain backup communication channels. Have manual overrides for automated systems. Cross-check algorithmic outputs with human judgment.

Technology is most valuable when it's redundant, not when it's singular.

4. Invest in technology that reduces optionality slowly

Some technology reduces your options—creates lock-in, path dependency, irreversibility. This can be dangerous in times of rapid change.

Favor technology that expands options or preserves flexibility. Distributed power systems give you optionality that grid dependence doesn't. Modular building systems allow adaptation in ways that integrated systems don't.

5. Remember that technology amplifies human choices

Ultimately, technology doesn't determine outcomes—it amplifies the consequences of human decisions. If our decisions prioritize short-term profit over long-term resilience, technology will help us extract that profit faster and more completely—right up until the system collapses. If our decisions prioritize genuine resilience and adaptation, technology can help us implement those decisions more effectively.

The technology is neutral. We're not.

Looking Forward

As we move toward Chapter 8's examination of societal transformation, keep this technological perspective in mind: we're living through the first climate crisis where nearly perfect information is available in real-time to nearly everyone.

This information transparency is going to accelerate social and economic changes in ways previous generations didn't experience. Climate migration, capital reallocation, insurance market transformation, property repricing—all of these will happen faster because information moves instantly.

The survivors won't be those with the best technology. They'll be those who use technology appropriately while understanding its limitations—who combine technological capability with human judgment, who deploy innovation while maintaining resilience.

I'm reminded of my earliest experience with Hurricane Andrew. The Weather Service had technology to track the storm, model its path, predict its intensity. That technology was valuable—it enabled our evacuation.

But what mattered in the aftermath wasn't the technology. It was the decisions people made: rebuild stronger or rebuild the same? Adapt or hope it won't happen again? Change behavior or cross fingers? The technology showed us the storm. It couldn't make us prepare for it.

Now let's look at how society itself is transforming in response to these intersecting forces—and what that means for where and how we'll live in the decades ahead.

III.

NAVIGATING A NEW FUTURE

CHAPTER 8

Riding the Wave of Societal Transformation

"History has reasons that reasons know nothing of."

\- BLAISE PASCAL

Now let's spend a few paragraphs looking at an aspect of history you probably didn't read about in your school textbooks, because I know I didn't. In fact, this perspective was borne from a business trip I took to Greece just a few years ago. The Greeks attribute a significant portion of the fall of their Athenian empire in the 400s BC to climate and weather. Repeatedly, as I walked the halls of the Acropolis Museum, I was faced with stories of famine, drought, and other climate-related disasters that played a major role in the Peloponnesian Empire's decline. It had me wondering whether the ten plagues documented in the Bible were actually climate events being interpreted by early human beings.

The United States stands nearly alone among developed nations in treating climate change as a matter of political opinion rather than observable fact. It's important to understand that climate is cyclical. I say this not to deny the effects of human industry on these cycles, but rather to point to facts of history. And humans have obviously played a role in speeding up Mother Nature's cycles.

My experience in Greece sent me down a rabbit hole to explore whether other major empires may have felt the effects of Earth's climate cycles. What I found was astonishing. The Dutch Empire, which reached far across our planet in the 17th and late 18th centuries, had several documented examples of climate instability. A Christmas Flood in 1717 killed thousands of people and started a cycle of devastating weather events that lasted for decades during the decline of the Dutch Empire. Cambridge University published a paper in 2022 about "Natural Disaster at the Closing of the Dutch Golden Era: Floods, Worms, and Cattle Plague." The volcanic eruption of Mount Tambora in 1815 in what was then known as the Dutch East Indies, caused global cooling in 1816 and created what history calls the "Year without a Summer."

By 1816, the British Empire had risen to power such that sun would never set. There were great famines in the late 19th century, as well as several examples of famine and drought. The British Empire did not fall primarily because of climate, but Mother Earth's influence was no joke.

In April of 2020, my then 14-year-old daughter and I loaded what we needed for a few weeks into a rented RV and headed west. Destination: Beverly Hills, California. We had planned to do a cross-country trip in the summer, hitting many of the national parks, but a pandemic altered our plans. As soon as we heard the remainder of my daughter's school year would be online, we hit the road. Visiting Federal lands was no longer an option. They had been shut down like everything else since the first outbreak hit. During a lockdown, we pulled up stakes altogether and moved from Florida to California. Aside from what we had with us in the RV, the rest of our worldly possessions were packed into a moving truck.

Every generation has defining moments. My parents remember JFK's assassination. My generation remembers 9/11. These events rewire how a society thinks about risk and vulnerability.

Every living person recalls the Covid lockdown of 2020 and those first few months of wild uncertainty and fear. Seemingly overnight, the context of our lives became survival mode. I remember calling my attorney in March to finalize my will, making sure I was adequately prepared to die. And I wasn't alone.

Catastrophic events can entirely upend the landscape of our lives. In the case of Covid, I am now the father of a daughter who didn't get to participate in her middle school graduation or experience her freshman year of high school in person. Freshman year of high school at Beverly Hills High (or any high school) can be hard enough, but Biz (her nickname) was the new kid in a new town, alone in her bedroom, zooming into a school where she knew no one. How weird that must have been for her, coping with a sense of displacement and social isolation? Making real connections in Tinsel Town is hard enough on a good day. I can't begin to fathom the long-term effects that year of online school had on kids of all ages.

Truth be told, though, it was my daughter's idea to up and move to California at the onset of the pandemic, and it was my bright idea to pay attention to her. She said, "Dad, let's get out of here. We should be somewhere else." And she was right. We were due for a change. As the rest of the world was burrowing into their homes, we fled ours for new pastures.

The RV rental was practically free, and our planned meandering excursion became a beeline from sea to shining sea. Everything was closed. The nation was masked, unpopulated, and unwelcoming. We rolled into Los Angeles like a post-apocalyptic version of the Beverly Hillbillies.

What strikes me about Covid now, looking back, is that we did roll with the punches. Every country in the world, stood strong in the face of unprecedented uncertainty and fear. It shows a resilience that humans have, one that creates hope we can survive the turbulent times ahead. Though nothing made sense at the time, we went into protection mode, followed the advice of the medical experts, wiped our groceries down with alcohol, and complied with isolation requirements. In retrospect, some of our behaviors were ridiculous, but the global society as a whole "went with it." We did what human beings have been doing since the dawn of time. We made do. We sacrificed. We moved, shifted, innovated, mourned, created, fell apart, banded together, adapted. We survived. (The cyclical nature of human existence is omnipresent in the pages of history.)

Change is inevitable. Whether it serves our individual interest, only history can tell.

We're all born assuming the world as we find it is the world as it's always been. The older we get, the harder it becomes to accept that it isn't. We favor our comforts, our routines, our nest eggs. But that desire for sameness flies in the face of every natural cycle on Earth.

The Covid Impact: Lifestyle Changes

One of the most significant behavioral shifts that occurred because of Covid was the dramatic and overnight movement from in-person activities to online everything. Beyond Zooming for school and work, the entire global economy went virtual. E-commerce exploded as anything anyone could conceive of buying, from a pencil to a penthouse, was showcased on websites, retailer apps, and through social media sites.

As someone who considers himself to be a relatively hip, in-the-know, cool dad (which is probably not something a real cool dad would say), I'm always fascinated when one of my own biases is exposed. I pride myself on looking at problems and challenges from all angles, being aware of forecasts and trends, and checking around doors most others don't consider. But until recently, I've been utterly blind to the volume of real estate transactions taking place on TikTok. When the reality of this situation penetrated, I went down a full-blown multi-leveled rabbit hole on the matter and discovered a vast shadow inventory of properties, sales transactions, and lending solutions that exist outside of what would now be considered the "traditional" real estate market.

This discovery led to three important realizations. 1. I'm getting old. 2. The younger generations are researching, shopping, comparing, negotiating, and purchasing in an entirely different way than their older counterparts, myself apparently among them. They refuse to do things the way their parents did. And 3. We, as a public, often can't see the headwinds coming straight at us because we're looking at the data from an old-world point of view, or getting lagging indicators, and we're missing key information.

For example, when it comes to the residential real estate market, my go-to resources are no doubt outdated, but they're familiar to me, and I'm not inclined to let go of them easily: the antiquated but utilitarian Multiple Listing System, Realtor.com or Zillow, and transaction details available from the traditional resources. When I speak with colleague members of the Mortgage Bankers Association, they speak of conventional mortgages, which represent only 60-70% of the actual mortgage market. They're not considering the shadow activity that represents a growing amount of private debt and huge volume of private real estate transactions. Until recently, I wasn't either.

Now that my eyes are open, I'm learning about new tech developments in my own space every day, such as travel to rent programs or swap to own programs. The private sector is always evolving and innovating, so when someone goes online to shop for mortgage rates, the private guys are right there to capture eyeballs and clicks. The changes in my industry are technology-related, and change is inevitable, whatever form it takes.

The Covid years were surprisingly difficult in my distressed debt buying business, the opposite of what many in private equity initially predicted. At the onset of the pandemic, I experienced the same feeling I usually get at the arrival of a hurricane: excitement mixed with resolve. The early hysteria and uncertainty, particularly around people's fluctuating employment status, meant they would need to re-evaluate their mortgages. In short, the mortgage industry would need guys like me to help them problem-solve their debt.

Instead, the government stepped in and took two key actions that altered the country's economic outlook. To avert mass hysteria, the Fed put a moratorium on government-insured mortgages being foreclosed and evictions were stopped. Mortgage loan servicers instituted forbearance and modification programs on the 70% of the residential mortgages that are US insured, and it's had effects on all types of loan servicing since then.

The second step the government took was to flood the American economy with money. Both administrations—first Trump, then Biden—doled out trillions in economic relief and stimulus, borrowed from other countries. Both presidencies and both Congresses injected unprecedented amounts of cash into the hands of its citizens and corporations, all in the name of preventing an economic collapse. We are now reaping the effects of all that free money and low interest rates in terms of inflation and asset bubbles.

But I digress. The point is, instead of Covid opening a new world of opportunities in my business, it had the opposite effect. Most of the non-performing loan inventory we've bought in the last fifteen years has been trickle-downs, either directly or indirectly, from Fannie, Freddie, Ginnie Mae, HUD, or the FHA. Many of my smart competitors pulled out in recent years, citing not enough distress in the market or dumb money paying over PAR for NPLs (meaning paying more than 100% of UPB for a defaulted loan).

Demographic Shifts

While the younger generations embrace tech and have new ways of doing things, the aging population and their shifting lifestyle priorities has been a topic in various industries for several decades. Each sector attempts to anticipate and capitalize on their patterns. Certainly, Covid fueled the flames but the Baby Boomers, the group of people born after World War II between 1946 to 1964, are aging, and their needs are changing.

If we think about market cycles in terms of generations, the Baby Boomers have experienced a period of unprecedented wealth accumulation. Sure, they've experienced a series of economic setbacks, specifically the painful Great Financial Crisis from 2007-09, the Dot Com Bubble Burst of 2001, the comparatively mild Gulf War recession of the early 90s, the Recession of 1980 followed by the Energy Crisis of 1981, and the Oil Embargo Recession from 1973-75.

See a pattern here? Roughly every eight to ten years, the Baby Boomers have had to weather economic downturns or periods of decline, some of which lasted longer than others. In fact, the Boomers have endured nearly a dozen recessions to date, with the average lasting about 15 months. Each recession has posed its own unique set of challenges, and some people lost their shirts, their houses, and their entire retirement nest egg. But overall, the Baby Boomers (now in their 70s and 80s) are the most prosperous and powerful generation on Earth. Boomers represent 20% of the US population but own more than 40% of US real estate, many being mom-and-pop landlords or owners of second and third homes.

A handful of the Boomers are very rich. Their parents experienced the scarcity of the Great Depression and the rationing of WWI and WWII, and there was no way these kids were going to save tin foil. They grew up in the Golden Age of Abundance and sit atop the gilded throne of the American Empire, having largely achieved the American Dream. These people look back with fondness on the way things used to be, and why not? They paid very little for their college degrees; they had long-term careers with stable companies, they bought houses for $50,000 that are worth ten times that today, they invested in their 401Ks, they diversified their portfolios and rode the stock market, they collected pensions and social security. They enjoy their Medicare, and they're not inclined to let go of a single shred of it.

The Boomers are in protection mode. Many of them believe the same tools and strategies, attitudes, and perspectives that aided them in the acquisition of their wealth 20 or 30 years ago will help them hang onto it. They've become complacent (kind of like Kodak), and they are reluctant to adopt new tools and strategies that are more appropriate for the volatility of today's market. This complacency is perfectly natural. The older we get, the harder it is to change.

The benefit of age is experience. Boomers have been riding the market waves all their lives. If they are willing to accept that change is coming and prepare for it, they will be able to protect what they've created. Since 2011, about 10,000 Americans a day have crossed age 65, and by 2030 every Baby Boomer will be at least that age. Zillow counted roughly 20.9 million empty-nest households in 2022. That doesn't mean 20.9 million turnkey homes are about to hit the market, but it does mean a massive housing reshuffling is coming. Most of that stock sits in suburbs and rural areas that younger buyers may not want, often in homes that need renovation or sit in climate-risk zones the original owners never had to price. The mainstream media keeps telling us we have a housing shortage. We don't have a pure shortage—we have a mismatch.

It will be harder on younger generations, who have only ever experienced a strong US economy, but who also face deep wealth disparity, rising costs of education, housing prices, and stagnant wages. Scott Galloway, professor of business and marketing at NYU and host of the Prof G podcast, speaks about these challenges in his newsletters and interviews. Scott delves into the systemic obstacles young people face, especially young men. He argues they are financially worse off than ever, citing data that specifies, "People over the age of 55 feel pretty good about America," whereas people over the age of 70 used to control 19 percent of household income versus people under the age of 40, used to control 12. Their wealth has been cut in half. This isn't by accident, it's purposeful." Galloway talks about these challenges in his newest book and has become a leading voice for macroeconomic changes necessary to help our next generation of millennials and beyond. The Federal Reserve's own Survey of Consumer Finances confirms the disparity: in 1989, households headed by someone under 35 held 21% of aggregate wealth. By 2022, that share had fallen to 6%. Meanwhile, the cost of a median home relative to median household income has nearly doubled since 1990. Young Americans aren't failing to build wealth because they lack ambition—the math has changed beneath their feet, and convergence will make it worse.

Evolving Housing Trends

Back in 2004 and 2005, developers in Florida built a large volume of super high-end, luxury senior living facilities in preparation for the influx of aging, wealthy, northern Boomers flocking south for retirement. It has long been baked into the Floridian consciousness that the state will be a mecca for retirees, and they would need somewhere to live when they got there. Miami, Naples, and Palm Beach were particularly popular regions for such growth. Unfortunately, the developers focused exclusively on the ultra-wealthy clientele, leaving a dearth of options for the average retiree, which remains a challenge to this day.

What the developers could not have anticipated was the volume of non-retirees who would also choose to move to Florida and other coastal regions because of Covid, putting further strain on an already tight housing market. Not only was there an influx of people fleeing the cities, but the entire way people viewed their homes changed, too. "Home" became much more than just a place to live; it became a place to work, to teach, to hide from disease in the outside world. Our homes became our sanctuaries.

One of the positives of the pandemic, for me, was a year of seeing my family on a regular basis. While many people were ready to kill family members, and I'm sure I had my moments, but overall, I loved it. It opened the idea that anyone could design a lifestyle of their choosing if they had a means to support it. Local was no longer necessary.

Prior to the Great Financial Crisis of 2008, the trend in residential housing was "bigger is better." It was the McMansion Era, and people were building 6,000, 10,000, and 15,000-square-foot single-family homes. Typically, these types of homes are found in communities where there is a concentration of wealth. Modern-day Pyramids now exist amid high-net-worth neighborhoods such as Beverly Hills and Bel Air, in coastal California towns such as Monterey and Malibu, dotting the shoreline of east coast old money bastions in Connecticut and Massachusetts, the mountains of Colorado in Aspen or Vail, and in the exclusive beach towns and barrier islands of Florida.

Due to what the average Americans went through in 2008, the trend bounced back to less gargantuan houses. Post GFC, people realized that 3,000 to 5,000 square feet was an adequately sized home to raise a family in, and Covid reinforced this desire to live less extravagantly. The GFC and Covid accelerated what was already happening from a demographic perspective: Baby Boomers retiring, downsizing, and moving to warmer climates. More on that later.

Today, we're seeing an amalgamation of housing trends in the market. Inventory for $3 million+ properties is starting to rise, but record-breaking residential prices still dot headlines of The Real Deal. I expect these higher end homes to bubble and pop first.

My daughter is going to college in Nevada, so I've been researching the real estate market in Las Vegas where I recently relocated. In 2024, 83 homes listed at $3 million or more sold. Prior to Covid in 2019, the highest number of houses that sold within that value range was 45. Today, there are more than 435 active listings of homes priced over $3 million within a 5-mile radius of the Las Vegas airport. Based on the past consumption rates for these types of properties, there is now a 10-year inventory of mega-mansions being speculatively sold or resold in Vegas, and that's just one market. A crisis in the jumbo market is brewing.

Just as developers look to the aging population to predict their needs, there has been equal speculation regarding the younger generations. What will their housing needs be? Do the younger generations even dream of home ownership, or have they been priced out of the American dream?

We see more and more 20- and 30-year-olds moving back in with their parents due to a variety of factors, such as rising rents and property values. Pew found that in 2023, 57% of adults ages 18 to 24 were living in a parent's home, and about a third of young adults overall were living with their parents. The trend is more pronounced in expensive metros, where the cost of living is higher, and it is feeding a growing demand for multi-generational housing.

The younger generations face a very different world than their elders. They're coming out of college saddled with thousands of dollars of debt and without job prospects that will help them make a dent in that debt. It's no wonder they do things differently than their parents. The world has changed. Circumstances, opportunities, and government programs, have changed, too. Not to mention the impact that AI may have on job markets.

Migratory Patterns & Remote Employment

I've been a remote worker for most of my life. While writing my first book, *Win-Win Revolution*, I lived in Florida and worked for a private equity firm in New York. Now, I live in California and run my mortgage and real estate investment platform from anywhere with an internet connection. What changed after Covid is that my situation stopped being unusual. Stanford's WFH Research estimates that as of 2025, work from home accounts for roughly a quarter of paid workdays among Americans ages 20 to 64. That is a seismic shift in the nation's employment patterns, and it helps explain why commercial real estate has not snapped back to its old equilibrium.

The traditional 9-to-5 office job has quickly become a thing of the past. The pandemic demonstrated that people no longer needed to be in the office to get their work done. Reluctantly, executives came to accept that most people have a higher level of motivation and productivity when they aren't faced with the added time suck of a daily commute. Though this is still being debated and there are productivity concerns now being raised, the work-from-home trend does allow greater flexibility.

The increase in remote work has caused an exodus out of and away from major cities. During and after Covid, those with remote positions have moved to more rural or coastal areas that afford a higher quality of life. And thus, the rise of vacancies in cities and small towns across America. As employees moved out, the homeless, displaced, and drug-addicted populations moved into city parks, abandoned buildings, temporary encampments, and subway stations. This reality created a ricochet effect of un-addressed societal issues, and now the cities are slowly rebounding to their vibrancy.

Some of our country's greatest cities, such as New York, Los Angeles, and San Diego, had an almost apocalyptic feeling about them. New York will always be New York, but it has not been im-mune to the societal shifts and changes that occurred post pandemic. By mid-2020, the exodus out of the city reached a noticea-ble level, particularly among higher-income families and individ-uals. They fled to the Hamptons or to second homes in Connect-icut, the Hudson Valley, and points beyond. At one point, amid declining tax revenue, New York Governor Andrew Cuomo be-gan begging the rich to return with a promise to fix crime, clean up graffiti, and help the homeless. "We'll go to dinner! I'll buy you a drink! Come over, I'll cook!" he promised.

Yet, as of this writing, office vacancies remain at dangerously high levels due to the shift of white-collar employment toward re-mote or hybrid work. The distress in this sector is not yesterday's news. The Mortgage Bankers Association reported in March 2026 that $875 billion of commercial mortgages are scheduled to mature in 2026 alone, including roughly $200 billion in CMBS, CLO, and other ABS loans. Office is not the whole problem, but it is a major part of the pressure. The ripple effect for cities such as New York is obvious: weaker buildings, weaker tax revenue, and weaker demand for the restaurants, retailers, and services that depend on full downtowns.

I moved to New York City at the age of 17 to start college, and The City will always hold a special place in my heart. Though New York looks and feels a lot different than it did in the '90s, I look forward to the return of excitement I felt there and have faith it will return in some manner once the commercial side of the equation has cycled through its decline.

The migratory shift out of cities and high-rent states is not exclusive to individuals. Several businesses have also decided to relocate. Elon Musk re-established his core base of operations for Tesla from Palo Alto, California, to Austin, Texas, in 2021. His reasons for the move were multi-fold. California has some of the highest income taxes in the country, whereas Texas does not have any state income tax at all, which means more cash for the company and its employees. Texas also boasts a significantly lower cost of living, which makes it easier to attract and retain talent. The Lone Star state has fewer regulations and more business-friendly incentives than California, where it is increasingly cost-prohibitive to own and operate a business. To Elon, the cost of relocating outweighed the cost to stay.

Though Tesla's move was highly publicized, Musk's company was far from a pioneer in this regard. Toyota moved its headquarters from Torrance, CA, to Plano, TX, in 2017. Mitsubishi relocated from Cypress, CA, to Franklin, TN, in 2019. Oracle left Redwood City, CA, for Austin, TX, in 2020, and Boeing moved from Puget Sound, WA, to Charleston, SC, in 2011. All of these moves were made to adapt to changing economic conditions, improving profitability, and to reduce costs by operating in states with better tax and incentives.

The migratory patterns of individuals and businesses speak volumes about shifting economic tides. I've been following these trends since the early 2000s largely because they offer clues about the real estate climate and how people are impacted by it. Societal transformations, such as large groups of people and companies moving from one location to another, are a clear indication that change is imminent, just as it was for me and my daughter when we loaded up the RV and headed to California. Though people and companies are leaving California in droves, I was one guy who made the opposite move. I love our major cities and believe that they are the heart and organs of any society.

I am the first to acknowledge that change is both constant and hard. Everyone craves stability and wants to stay in the bubble of the boom time. But societal changes, demographic power shifts, and rapidly evolving economic and real estate markets are a fact of life. To navigate and thrive through these choppy waters, individuals, investors, regulators, bankers, and policymakers must adopt a proactive and adaptive mindset. They must reach across the aisle and seize the opportunity to reshape our cities by addressing new infrastructure requirements for the next hundred years versus just waiting for the next bridge to collapse and focusing on immediate problems. By embracing technological advancements, we can build the cities and towns of tomorrow that will serve our future civilization more efficiently and effectively. More of this transformation will be discussed in later chapters.

CHAPTER 9

When Play Breaks Down, Find a Coach

*"In theory, theory and practice are the same.
In practice, they are not."*

—YOGI BERRA

The call came on a Tuesday morning in March 2023. I recognized the number—the regional president of a bank I'd worked with during the 2008 crisis. We'd stayed in touch over the years, the way you do with fellow financial warriors.

"Bill, we've got a situation," he said, skipping pleasantries. "Actually, 23 situations."

He was referring to 23 commercial properties in his portfolio—mostly in coastal Florida and Louisiana. Five years earlier, when his bank underwrote these loans, they looked like textbook-perfect deals: strong borrowers, solid properties, conservative loan-to-value, adequate insurance coverage, and sensible debt service coverage ratios.

Then the convergence started.

Insurance companies started leaving these markets. The remaining carriers tripled premiums. Property values softened as buyers factored in the new insurance reality. And now, all 23 loans were approaching their maturity dates—which meant refinancing at interest rates often double the original terms, in markets where lenders were getting increasingly nervous about climate exposure.

His internal Special Assets Group was drowning. They knew how to handle straightforward defaults—borrower mismanagement, market downturns, fraud. They didn't know how to handle convergence crises where the real estate, the insurance market, and the financing all broke simultaneously.

"You've seen this before," he said. "What do we do?"

Actually, I hadn't seen this before—not exactly. The 2008 crisis was about leverage, fraud, and unqualified folks getting 100% loans. These were good properties, good borrowers, doing everything right. The system itself had shifted beneath them.

But I had seen enough cycles, worked through enough distressed situations, developed enough unconventional strategies to know that when banks call in outside help, it's not because they lack intelligence or resources. It's because they need someone who can see the problem differently—someone who isn't constrained by internal policies written for normal times, who can try things that would never survive an internal credit committee.

Why Banks Struggle with Convergence

Banks aren't bad at managing distressed debt because they hire the wrong people. Their people are smart, dedicated, and experienced within their domain. The limitation is structural, baked into how banks are designed to operate.

Banks are masterworks of standardization. Their ability to process thousands of transactions daily depends on consistent procedures, clear approval hierarchies, and replicable processes. This architecture serves them exceptionally well under normal circumstances. It becomes a liability when each troubled loan is a unique puzzle with interlocking pieces.

I learned this firsthand in the 2008 crisis after being invited into a Midwest bank to assess 400 non-performing loans on their books. Their internal loss mitigation team had three people trying to manage all 400—plus their regular duties. Each loan needed three to five hours per week of focused attention. That's 1,200 hours of work per week for a team with 120 hours of capacity. They were drowning, making decisions based on urgency rather than optimal outcome. Defaulting to foreclosure because it was the only solution they had to execute at scale, immediately.

Convergence makes this problem exponentially harder. A traditional default has one diagnosis: the borrower can't pay. A convergence crisis has five diagnoses tangled together—the real estate is fundamentally sound, but insurance has become unaffordable, the borrower is performing but can't refinance, the property could be viable, but climate risk has repriced the entire market. You can't solve these with a single department's playbook because no single department owns the whole problem.

Here's the part that keeps coming back to haunt us: after the 2008 crisis wound down and defaults went to zero, most banks dismantled their Special Assets Groups. Everyone did. It made sense at the time. But what they lost was not a department. They lost institutional memory. The workout specialists who could restructure a loan creatively, who could sit across from a frightened borrower and find a path forward—those people retired or moved in the private sector. The analysts who replaced them have never operated in a normal rate environment, let alone a crisis.

The Integration Problem

The hardest part of convergence scenarios isn't solving individual problems—it's solving them simultaneously and accounting for how solutions to one problem affect the others.

You can solve an insurance problem by reducing coverage limits. But that affects the bank's collateral position. Which affects the refinancing terms available. Which affects the property's cash flow viability. Which loops back to insurance affordability.

Or you can solve a financing problem by extending the loan term. The Fed gave banks a new set of tools in recent years. Concerned rising delinquencies too quickly influencing the bank's regulatory capital requirements, the Fed created TDR and CECL guidelines that allowed them to effectively rewrite the terms of any loan to any level just to maintain its accrual (performing) status. The industry has a phrase for it as we've previously discussed: extend and pretend. This all circles back to whether the loan or the relationship are worth trying to save at all.

Specialization often creates additional hinderances to resolving any non-performing, sub-performing scenario. Internal bank teams, organized into specialized departments, struggle with these circular dependencies. Credit analysts focus on credit. Legal focuses on documentation. Asset managers focus on operations. The integration happens in committee meetings where no one has the full picture.

Outside advisors, working on a specific portfolio of troubled loans, can see and manage these interconnections because it's their entire focus. Third party advisors are not trying to fit convergence problems into departmental silos—they build holistic solutions that account for how all the pieces interact. They bring networks that don't exist inside the bank—connections to specialty insurance markets, subordinated climate-risk lenders, municipal pilot programs, and alternative capital sources that bankers are unaware of.

Liquidity is the key component. I'd be remiss having written this entire book without addressing the liquidity crunch we are now seeing since the recent rise in interest rates. There has been so much cash sloshing around the system for the past decade that it created the many asset bubbles we see today, not just in real estate but all asset classes.

And no economist or market maker can possibly predict the exact timing that macro-economic liquidity becomes an issue. We are seeing the system being drained of capital. Private Equity is reeling, the Fed is lowering its balance sheet monthly, and US trade deficits remain in the wrong direction. Our federal government has not lowered spending. Recent efficiency initiatives have not meaningfully reduced spending, and with military commitments around the world, we continue to rack up greater national debt through deficit spending.

Where this really becomes a problem is in the servicing of our U.S. national debt. As of March 2026, gross federal debt is about $38.9 trillion, the average interest rate on marketable debt is about 3.36%, and net interest is on track to exceed defense spending in 2026. New U.S. debt issuance is still pricing in the 4s and 5s, which means our interest bill is likely to keep climbing even if the total debt stops growing. The patient may soon be our own USG.

What a Convergence Workout Looks Like

One property in that 23-loan portfolio shows how a solution plays out in practice.

The property: 42,000 square feet of retail and office space, three blocks from Fort Lauderdale beach. Built in 2015, well-maintained, 92% occupied. Borrower had never missed a payment. Original loan: $6.2 million at 3.75%, maturing in August 2024.

Then the convergence: Insurance renewed in 2023 at $128,000—up from $44,000 the year before. Three commercial tenants gave notice due to their own insurance difficulties. Property value declined from $8.8 million to $7.2 million due to climate risk repricing and a declining NOI. Refinancing required the deal to work at 7.5% rates, which the property's income couldn't support. And the city indicated a major stormwater infrastructure assessment was coming—estimated at $180,000.

The bank's initial approach: require the borrower to pay down principal or face foreclosure. Standard playbook. But the borrower didn't have a million dollars to inject, and foreclosure would force the bank to take ownership of a property with unsustainable insurance costs, declining value, and infrastructure liabilities. The bank's own recovery in foreclosure would be worse than keeping the loan.

The workout combined elements no internal credit committee would have assembled on its own: insurance restructuring through Citizens Property Insurance that brought costs down to $89,000; $185,000 in physical improvements—upgraded drainage, wind-resistant features—that qualified the property for better rates over time; lease restructuring with remaining tenants who got improvement allowances in exchange for longer terms; a modified loan at $5.8 million at 6.75% plus a $200,000 subordinated note from a specialty lender who understood climate-adapted properties; and a negotiated arrangement with the city for the borrower to participate in a pilot program for climate-adaptive infrastructure.

The result: property stabilized, occupancy increased to 96% within eight months as climate-resistant features attracted tenants leaving less-adapted buildings. The bank maintained a performing loan. The borrower preserved ownership and improved the asset. None of the individual pieces were revolutionary. The integration was what mattered—seeing how insurance, physical improvements, tenant strategy, financing, and municipal coordination could be woven into a single solution.

Twenty-One Out of Twenty-Three

By the end of that engagement, 21 of the 23 troubled loans were restructured and performing. The two we couldn't save were already so far underwater that orderly liquidation was the only path—but even there, the recovery was 78% versus the bank's internal estimate of 65%.

That portfolio would have generated $14.7 million in losses under the bank's internal approach. With specialized intervention: $3.8 million. The delta—$10.9 million—dwarfed the advisory fees by a factor of two hundred.

I share these numbers not to sell you on third-party advisory—though I'll be transparent: my firm does this work, and we're good at it. I've built a career on the belief that distressed debt resolution done right serves everyone—the borrower keeps a roof, the bank preserves capital, and the community avoids another boarded-up building. That dual purpose—doing well by doing good—isn't a marketing line. It's the only model I've seen that actually works over multiple cycles. I share these numbers because they illustrate something important about where we are: the problems facing banks and borrowers in this convergence are solvable, but they're not solvable with the tools and structures designed for the last crisis. The playbooks need to be rewritten for a world where real estate, insurance, climate, and financing all break simultaneously.

Whether that rewriting happens inside the bank or with outside help is less important than the fact that it happens. And yes, I have a stake in this conversation—my firm exists precisely to fill this gap. But I wrote this book because the problem is bigger than any one firm's capacity. The industry needs hundreds of qualified workout teams, not just mine. If this book persuades a single bank to rebuild its internal SAG before the next wave of maturities, that serves the public interest regardless of who does the work. Banks that rebuild workout capacity with people who have cycle experience, who understand climate-adjacent markets, who can see the integration problem clearly—those banks will navigate this convergence. Banks that wait for the old playbook to start working again will find themselves, like my friend's bank in 2023, staring at a portfolio of 23 problems they don't have the tools to solve.

As convergence scenarios become more common, the ability to see across silos—to integrate real estate expertise with insurance knowledge with climate science with creative finance—becomes the decisive capability. However institutions develop that capability, the ones who have it will manage through. The ones who don't will be managed by someone else.

But what many people assume will solve our problems when banks and advisors can't is good old government intervention. As we move into Chapter 10, we'll examine that assumption. Because if you're counting on government rescue when the convergence intensifies, I've got some disappointing news based on decades of watching government respond to financial crises.

CHAPTER 10

The Room Where it Happens

*"Government is not the solution to our problem;
government is the problem..."*
—RONALD REAGAN

"...unless it's your bank that's failing."
—MOST CAPITALISTS I KNOW

In the fall of 2008, I attended a Skype call with a group of bankers and private equity managers who sat nervously inside their Midtown Manhattan conference rooms. Six months earlier, they were the most confident people in any room. They wore custom suits. They quoted Ayn Rand. They believed, with religious conviction, that free markets self-corrected and government intervention was the enemy of prosperity.

This afternoon, they were begging for a bailout.

I watched one managing director—a man who had lectured me over dinner about the evils of regulation not three months prior—literally plead with a Treasury Department liaison for access to TARP funds. His firm had leveraged itself forty-to-one on mortgage-backed securities, and the music had stopped. The ideology of free markets evaporated the moment his personal net worth was on the line.

I don't tell this story to mock my friends. Rather it reveals something fundamental about how we relate to government intervention: we're against it in theory and desperate for it in practice. We want free markets when we're winning and a safety net when struggling. We privatize gains and socialize losses and act surprised when any cycle repeats.

I've lived through several major government rescues in my career—the Savings & Loan crisis resolution of the early '90s (albeit I was a student at the time) and the massive bailouts of the 2008 Great Financial Crisis, both related to banking and real estate. I worked on deals directly affected by TARP, participated in programs designed to stabilize housing markets, and advised clients navigating government workout initiatives. I witnessed politicians making promises, regulators scrambling to implement programs, and taxpayers constantly footing bills they never anticipated.

Here's what I learned: government intervention in financial crises is inevitable, usually necessary, and almost always imperfect. The question isn't when and whether government will intervene as this convergence crisis intensifies. More importantly, how effectively and who will pay the ultimate price.

A Pattern as Old as the Republic

America has been bailing out its financial system since before most of us were born. The pattern is remarkably consistent: a period of deregulation and easy money breeds excessive risk-taking and overlooked vulnerability. Then a crisis hits. Government intervenes with emergency measures. Reforms are enacted. Then, gradually, the reforms are rolled back, memory fades, and the cycle begins again. We've been running on this hamster wheel since 1929.

After the Great Depression vaporized the savings of millions and shuttered thousands of banks, the government responded with the most comprehensive financial intervention in history. The Glass-Steagall Act separated commercial from investment banking. The FDIC was created to guarantee deposits. The SEC was established to police securities markets. And the Reconstruction Finance Corporation—the RFC—was deployed to stabilize a failing banking system.

The RFC is worth pausing on because it represents something rare in government intervention: a program that worked well and then went away. Created in 1932 under Hoover and expanded under Roosevelt, the RFC provided direct loans to struggling banks and businesses when private credit had evaporated. It was massive in scope—at its peak, it was arguably the most powerful financial institution in the world. But it was designed with an expiration date. It had clear mandates, transparent operations, and a directive to return markets to private function. And here's the part that should make every modern policymaker blush: the RFC returned a profit to taxpayers. Roughly $500 million—about $11 billion in today's dollars—was returned to public coffers by the time it was dissolved in 1957.

The Resolution Trust Corporation followed that same discipline in the 1980s. When over a thousand S&Ls collapsed under the weight of deregulation-fueled speculation and outright fraud, Congress created the RTC with a specific, time-limited mission—take over the failed institutions, liquidate the assets, and shut itself down. The RTC handled assets from 747 failed institutions with a book value exceeding $400 billion in today's money. About forty percent of those assets were commercial real estate—a close parallel to what's sitting on regional bank balance sheets right now. Taxpayers still absorbed roughly $160 billion in losses. But the RTC was focused, temporary, and accountable. It resolved the crisis without creating another permanent government fixture. And it bred an entire new generation of millionaires and billionaires smart enough to pounce on the opportunities that arose out of its ashes.

What the RFC and the RTC had in common was discipline: a clear mandate, a sunset provision, and the humility to leverage private expertise rather than pretending public servants could manage thousands of distressed assets better than private professionals.

Then came the Great Financial Crisis, and we lost that discipline. TARP, the emergency lending facilities, the conservatorship of Fannie Mae and Freddie Mac, the backdoor bailout of AIG—these were not temporary bridges back to private function. They were permanent alterations to the relationship between government and financial markets. The Fed opened the discount window at zero cost and left it there for fourteen years. Fannie and Freddie were placed in conservatorship in 2008. As of this writing, they're still there. Seventeen years and counting, with no clear plan for exit.

The interventions of 2008 prevented catastrophic collapse—I need to be clear about that. Without TARP and the Fed's extraordinary measures, the financial system might have imploded completely. Millions more would have lost their homes, their jobs, their savings. But saving the patient is not the same as curing the disease. We stabilized our system without addressing the underlying pathologies. We bailed out institutions that had profited from unsustainable practices and then allowed them to return to those same practices once the crisis passed, albeit under new names like RTL and DSCR. We created a generation of bankers and investors who internalized a dangerous lesson: take the risk, keep the upside, and if it blows up, the government will be there with a check.

That's a moral hazard, an injustice to the next generation, and it's the single biggest reason the convergence we're facing now will be harder to resolve than anything that came before.

The Dinner I Wish I Could Host

I've been turning a fantasy over in my mind for years. Imagine hosting a dinner—not a gala, not a fundraiser—just a table for four at a quiet restaurant in Fort Lauderdale, somewhere on Las Olas where the boats pass slowly and nobody's in a rush. My three guests: someone from the Fed, a senior Senator from the Banking Committee, and my neighbor Maria, a retired teacher who has lived in the same house east of I-95 for thirty-one years. We eat, we drink a good bottle of wine, and we talk about what's really happening.

In my head, this dinner has happened a hundred times, that I was finally in the room where it happened. Lying awake at three in the morning running scenarios, sitting through continuing education classes, driving home from meetings where smart people seemed to be talking past each other—I always end up back at this table, wishing I could get these three people in the same room. Because the gap between the people who control the levers, the people who write the rules, and the people who live with the consequences has never been wider. And that gap is where crises grow.

So let me tell you how the dinner goes.

• • •

We'd start with the Fed official. I'd pour the wine, let the pleasantries settle, and then I'd say what I've wanted to say for years: Thank you for 2008. You saved the patient. But you left the IV running for a bit too long, and now the patient is addicted to the drug.

We'd recall seeing how developers started building projects that only penciled at 3% CAP rates, how private equity has loaded companies with debt because the carrying cost seems negligible, and how non-performing loan pools went from thirty cents on the dollar in 2009 to almost PAR by 2019—not because the underlying assets improved, but because cheap leverage made every bet look rational. We watched an entire generation of bankers come of age believing that free capital was a permanent feature of the US economy.

Perhaps you should've started raising rates when we were printing trillions in COVID stimulus. Here's what I'd ask the Fed official to consider, over the second glass of wine:

Intervention must be designed to end. The RFC understood this. Jesse Jones ran it with a simple discipline—provide what the private market cannot, do it transparently, and leave when conditions allow. Compare that to Fannie and Freddie, still in conservatorship seventeen years later. This must be dealt with. If the Fed's balance sheet is still loaded with troubled loans or securities, let's create a short-term plan to liquidate those assets.

Some failures must be allowed to occur. I know that sounds cold over dinner. But when every bet gets backstopped, the message to every ambitious banker in the country is that the upside is theirs and the downside belongs to taxpayers. That's corrosive. It breeds the exact recklessness that creates the next crisis.

Monetize taxpayer assets whenever possible. The RFC returned $11 billion in today's dollars to the public. The RTC maximized recovery through private partnerships. If citizens are going to absorb risk, they deserve to share in the upside. That's not socialism—it's good deal-making.

• • •

Then I'd turn to Maria. Her husband was once Mayor of a small town called Margate. She is a retired teacher, widowed, living on a pension and small investment account that her husband setup when times were good. Maria is the person at the table who represents the ninety-eight percent of Americans who never fly private nor ski in Davos and Aspen. Maria bought her house in 1994 for $127,000 and has watched its Zillow value climb to $685,000, considering it a part of her retirement account even though she'll never sell. The house is paid off.

Florida has been booming in recent years, especially since COVID thrust thousands of new habitants to the area, many with wall street money seeking the haven of no state income tax and sunshine 300 plus days a year. For the locals, it seemed like a boom, new business popping up in areas of South Florida that had been sleepy and sluggish for years.

Maria asks us what to do now about the costs. Her fixed income from pension and social security serve basic needs, such as food, transportation, and health care costs. She's lived through decades of hurricane seasons paying into insurance programs. Then three years ago, her insurance started doubling, annually. Last year, basic coverage premiums topped $10,000 and she's now asking us at the table if she should let it lapse and take her chances. I blurt out, "absolutely not." But I immediately understand her impulse. When you're on a fixed income and your insurance triples, the math gets brutal.

It becomes an interesting conversation when both the Fed person and the Senator suggest she self-insure. Maybe they're right and Maria only can consider such an option since she has no mortgage. If she invested $10,000 a year herself into a "rainy day fund" she might be better suited. But this is a gamble reserved for few, now being sought out of desperation by many otherwise undercapitalized to take such risks.

I'd tell Maria to do what the professionals call a stress test—a kitchen-table version. Sit down with an honest spreadsheet. What happens if your insurance premium doubles again? If you lost your income source for six months or suffered a health concern, how long could you sustain your current obligations?

The others at the table both admit that they hear Maria's story almost every day and are quietly worrying themselves that so few Americans have a plan or a safety net.

We all agree from decades of watching communities navigate crises: the ones that organize before the storm consistently fare better than the ones that wait for Washington. When people pool information and coordinate early, they negotiate better with insurers, advocate more effectively with local government, and make smarter decisions about whether to stay, adapt, or relocate. Community resilience is not a slogan. It's a practical advantage.

Maria is a grandparent now and she brings these conversations to the dinner table with them. Teach them about financial resilience with the same urgency she taught them about education and health. The economy they will inherit is being shaped right now.

• • •

Finally, we'd turn to the Senator. I'd refill their glass and say something that probably wouldn't go over well at a campaign event: you have advance notice this time, and advance notice is the rarest gift in politics.

About $875 billion of commercial mortgages are scheduled to mature in 2026 alone—much of it originated during the cheap-money era at rates and valuations that no longer reflect reality. Regional banks are concentrated in this paper. Insurance markets are retreating from entire regions. Reinsurance is an opaque business that we cannot fully rely on. Debt levels beyond real estate are a ticking time bomb. The timeline is not theoretical. It's published in lenders' maturity schedules, call reports, and in the actions of private equity firms gating redemptions.

Congress almost never gets to see the iceberg before the ship hits it. This time, you can. The maturity wall is not a surprise. Private Credit is the canary in the coal mine. Insurance markets fracturing is no surprise. Climate costs compounding on coastal and wildfire-prone assets is certainly no surprise. This crisis is approaching on schedule, perhaps slower than Al Gore predicted, and in a degree, we can manage if we act.

I'd put three requests on the table:

1. **First, authorize and capitalize a resolution entity now**—before the first wave of bank failures forces an emergency vote. Model it on the RTC but fund it in advance. Give it a charter, a sunset date, and the authority to partner with private sector asset managers the day it's needed. The worst time to design a rescue program is in the middle of a panic, when every lobbyist in Washington is rewriting the legislation to protect their clients.

2. **Second, write claw back provisions into statute.** Not guidelines, not best practices—statute. Any private insti-

tution that receives public rescue funds should trigger automatic compensation claw backs for senior executives. After 2008, the American public watched institutions that created the crisis emerge with their executive compensation structures largely intact. If you want behavior to change, consequences must exist. Citizens like Maria deserve accountability.

3. **Third, leverage private expertise rather than expanding government's operational footprint.** The RTC didn't try to manage thousands of distressed properties with federal employees. It created the framework, set the rules, and let experienced professionals execute. That model works. Conservatorship—where government holds assets indefinitely without a clear exit strategy—does not.

The Senator admits, now a few glasses down, that pre-funding a resolution entity means acknowledging a crisis before it arrives. Statutory claw backs make enemies of donors. Sunset provisions mean giving up future leverage in Congress. The frankness is admirable. And this convergence needs leadership now. Perhaps everyone's listening for once.

· · ·

Why the Old Playbook Won't Be Enough

The wine's gone. Dessert's been cleared. And now I'd say the thing that ties it all together—the thing I'd want all three of my dinner guests to hear at the same time, because it's the thing that none of them can solve alone.

What makes this moment different—and what makes me less certain that the old intervention playbook will work—is the convergence factor. Previous crises were primarily financial in nature. The economy was fundamentally sound; it just needed to get past the panic. The RFC could stabilize Depression-era banks because the American economy had enormous productive capacity waiting to be unlocked. The RTC could liquidate S&L assets because those assets had real value in stable markets. Even TARP could flood the system with cheap money because, once housing stabilized, the broader economy could resume growth. The COVID bailouts, on the other hand, may someday be remembered as the greatest gift the Baby Boomers could ever give themselves, courtesy of their grandchildren. Our national debt, which fiscal conservatives once obsessed over, now stands near $38.9 trillion. More than $10 trillion of additional gross debt has been layered on over the past five years. I call it The Great Vacation, funded by all of us collectively, but put on the tab of future generations.

This time, the crisis isn't purely financial. It's structural. Climate volatility is permanently repricing assets in ways that no lending facility can reverse. Insurance markets are retreating from entire regions based on actuarial math that won't change with a policy shift. Demographic patterns are transforming where and how people live and work. Geopolitical unrest is rising and the USA has more enemies.

Today, we're staring at that $3 trillion maturity wall. Our federal government has not been so successful as we'd hoped in lowering spending. We continue to rack up greater national debt. As discussed in Chapter 9, our interest payments on national debt already exceed military spending—and that's at median rates around 3.5%. New issuance at 4-5% means the bill only grows from here.

Government intervention will come. It always does. And it may help at the margins—preventing the worst-case systemic collapse, providing some relief to the most affected communities, perhaps creating a modern version of the RTC to work through distressed bank portfolios. If we're fortunate, policymakers will study the models that worked and build something temporary, transparent, and accountable.

But government intervention will not stop the convergence. We cannot reverse sea-level rise or extend the life of infrastructure designed for a climate that no longer exists. We cannot compress a generational demographic shift into a quarterly earnings cycle or a quick band-aid from Uncle Sam. We need to think more long term, like societies that plan to be around for thousands more years.

In my fantasy, the dinner ends the way good dinners do— slowly, reluctantly, with the feeling that something was said that mattered. The Fed Official goes back to Washington with a practitioner's perspective they can't get from models. The Senator goes back to the Hill knowing that a constituent can articulate exactly what's coming and wants to be part of some solution. And Maria goes home believing that tomorrow may make the difference.

Of course, this perfect dinner hasn't happened. It probably won't. The people who control the levers, the people who write the rules, and the people who live with the consequences almost never sit at the same table.

I began this chapter talking about the banker begging for TARP funds in that Midtown conference room. He was a smart person. Sophisticated. Well-resourced. And yet, when the crisis hit, his first instinct was to look to someone else for rescue.

The path forward requires something no government can provide: individual resilience, institutional adaptation, and societal reconciliation. Real conversation outside of politics and personal agenda, a willingness to see the world as it is and build accordingly, rather than as we wish it were.

In the final chapter, we propose solutions. Because the best intervention isn't the one the government provides after the crisis. It's the one you build for yourself before it arrives.

CHAPTER 11

Building Resilient Systems

"The pessimist complains about the wind. The optimist expects it to change. The realist adjusts the sails."

—WILLIAM ARTHUR WARD

The Storm We're Already In

In the introduction to this book, I told you about Hurricane Andrew—how my family evacuated inland, how we watched the storm on television, how we returned to find our neighborhood damaged but standing. I told you about volunteering in the aftermath, seeing entire communities reduced to matchsticks, understanding for the first time the raw power of convergent forces.

What I didn't tell you then, because you weren't ready to hear it, is that the real lesson of Andrew wasn't about the storm itself. It was about what happened afterward.

In the weeks and months that followed, I watched two very different responses unfold. Some people rebuilt exactly what they had before—same elevation, same construction methods, same assumptions about what "normal" hurricanes looked like. Others rebuilt differently. They elevated their homes. They upgraded to impact-resistant windows and reinforced roof connections. They diversified their insurance. They changed their landscaping. They installed backup generators and water storage.

Both groups faced the same storm. Both experienced similar damage. But when the next storms came—and they always come—the outcomes were radically different.

The people who rebuilt to the old standard got hit harder each time. Their insurance premiums skyrocketed. Some couldn't get coverage at all. When they tried to sell, buyers factored in the risk. Eventually, some of them left Florida entirely, taking losses they could have avoided.

The people who rebuilt with resilience in mind weathered subsequent storms better. Their insurance remained manageable because they'd reduced their risk profile. Their property values held because buyers recognized the value of preparation. They didn't escape every impact, but they absorbed the shocks and recovered faster.

The difference between these two groups wasn't resources or luck. It was mindset.

One group asked: "How do I get back to normal?"

The other asked: "How do I build for the world that's actually coming?"

This chapter is about that second question.

Why Resilience Over Prediction

I've spent this entire book analyzing cycles, examining data, and making the case that we're heading toward significant economic disruption. Some readers might expect me to end with predictions: "The crisis will hit in Q3 2026" or "Commercial real estate will decline by X%."

I'm not going to do that. Here's why.

In complex systems experiencing convergence, precision is impossible and resilience is everything. Ray Dalio teaches us to think in probabilities, not certainties. What are the odds that commercial real estate faces stress in the next three to five years as debt matures and climate costs rise? Very high. What are the odds it happens on a specific date in a specific way? Impossible to know.

The weatherman can tell you a hurricane is forming in the Atlantic. They can project its general path with reasonable confidence. But they can't tell you with precision where it will make landfall. Does that uncertainty mean you don't prepare? Of course not. You prepare precisely because you can't predict with certainty.

Stop trying to predict the unpredictable. Start building systems that can handle a range of outcomes.

Start with why. Why does resilience matter more than prediction? Because resilience protects you when you're wrong. If I predict the crisis hits in 2026 and you position entirely for that timeline, what happens if it comes in 2025 or 2028 or unfolds gradually? Resilience protects you across all those scenarios. Resilience creates optionality—when you're resilient, you can respond to opportunities that emerge during transitions while the non-resilient are forced to react desperately. And resilience compounds: each resilient decision makes the next one easier, each vulnerability you address strengthens the whole system.

Four Pillars of Resilience

Before we get to strategies, we need a shared definition. Too often, "resilience" gets used vaguely to mean "strong" or "prepared." Real resilience is more specific.

To me, resilience means you can take a hit, adjust quickly, and keep moving forward without catastrophic loss.

Absorption Capacity

Can you absorb shocks without breaking? This is about buffers—financial reserves, insurance coverage, diversification, redundancy in critical systems. In real estate terms: can your property handle a 50% increase in insurance costs? Can you service your debt if rates increase 200 basis points? Can you withstand a 20% vacancy spike for six months? If the answer to any of these is no, you're fragile, and there's room to be more resilient.

Adaptive Capacity

Can you adjust your strategy when conditions change? This is about flexibility—avoiding lock-in to assumptions that may not hold, maintaining options, being able to pivot. Are you so leveraged that you can't exit positions if needed? Are you locked into long-term commitments based on assumptions about stable climate or low rates? Rigid systems break under stress. Adaptive systems bend and reshape. Optionality is key.

Transformative Capacity

Can you emerge from crisis fundamentally stronger? The developers who built Babcock Ranch in Florida didn't just build hurricane-resistant homes—they built an entirely new model for climate-resilient development that's now commanding premium prices and outperforming the market. They used the challenge of climate volatility to create something better than what existed before. That's transformative capacity.

Systemic Resilience

Can you build resilience not just for yourself but for the systems you depend on? If your property is resilient but the electrical grid isn't, you're still vulnerable. If your portfolio is strong but your banks are fragile, you're still at risk. True resilience requires thinking systemically strengthening not just your position but the ecosystem you operate within.

The Five-Layer Defense

Think of resilience like a medieval castle's defenses. You don't rely on just the walls or just the moat—you build multiple layers so that if one fails, others hold. Here is a practical framework that applies whether you're an institutional investor with billions under management or an individual with a few rental properties.

Layer 1: Asset Selection and Diversification

Your first line of defense is what you own and how you spread risk. Diversify across climate risk profiles—if 80% of your portfolio is in coastal Florida and Louisiana, you don't have diversification, you have concentration. True diversification means spreading across different climate vulnerabilities so no single event can take down your entire portfolio. Stagger debt maturity dates so you're never refinancing everything in the same twelve-month window. And think forward, not backward—markets that performed well over the past decade may be the most vulnerable in the next one. The Sunbelt migration fueled growth in Phoenix, Austin, and Miami, but those same markets now face water scarcity, extreme heat, and insurance crises. The Rust Belt cities that struggled may become more attractive as climate refugees seek cooler, water-rich environments.

Layer 2: Capital Structure and Liquidity

The era of maximizing leverage is over. In a convergent crisis, high leverage is high fragility. Target 40–50% loan-to-value instead of

70–80%. Keep 12 to 18 months of operating expenses and debt service in reserves. Favor longer-term, fixed-rate debt—every time I see an investor taking three-year floating-rate debt to maximize current returns, I know they're optimizing for today while ignoring tomorrow. Lock in longer terms. Yes, you'll pay more now. But you won't face a refinancing crisis in year three when rates have spiked and lending has tightened.

Layer 3: Operating Resilience

This is day-to-day management that reduces vulnerability: fixed-price contracts for insurance, utilities, and key services wherever you can eliminate volatility; redundancy in critical systems—backup generators, water storage, alternative suppliers; efficiency improvements that reduce operating costs and climate exposure simultaneously; and strong tenant relationships built on loyalty rather than maximum extraction. In a downturn, the properties that maintain occupancy are those where tenants feel valued.

Layer 4: Risk Transfer and Insurance

Over-insure relative to minimum requirements when premiums are low. Explore parametric insurance that pays out automatically when objective triggers are met—wind speed over a threshold, rainfall over a limit—bypassing the delays of claims adjustment. For larger portfolios, captive insurance structures let you self-insure with the tax benefits and risk management framework of traditional coverage. The insurance market is fracturing, and the investors who get creative about risk transfer now will have options when others don't.

Layer 5: Physical and Environmental Resilience

Retrofit for climate resilience: elevation, flood barriers, impact-resistant windows, enhanced roof connections, wildfire-resistant landscaping. A property owner in Fort Lauderdale spent $200,000 elevating his building and upgrading to Category 5 standards. His insurance premium dropped from $18,000 to $8,000 annually. The payback period was twenty years on premium savings alone—but he also increased the property value and reduced catastrophic loss risk. Design for passive survivability: can the building maintain livable conditions without power or water? Invest in green infrastructure—bioswales, cool roofs, rain gardens, pervious paving—that reduce flood risk and lower operating costs. And future-proof for regulation: the properties that comply with tomorrow's standards today avoid costly retrofits later.

Different Roles, Same Imperative

Resilience looks different depending on your seat at the table. For individual property owners, it starts with understanding your actual exposure—go to FirstStreet.org and get objective data on your climate risk, review your insurance coverage and refinancing dates, calculate whether you can absorb the shocks I've described in this book. Build reserves, implement quick-win improvements, and if you're heavily concentrated in high-risk areas, honestly assess whether that concentration still makes sense.

For investors and fund managers, it means integrating climate into underwriting as a core element rather than a compliance checkbox. Stress test your portfolio under scenarios where a major hurricane, a wildfire season, and a rate spike happen in the same year. Set resilience targets alongside return targets. Be transparent with your investors about exposure—they're sophisticated enough to understand risk, and what they need from you is honesty about it.

For developers, the decisions you make today determine whether the assets you create will appreciate or become stranded over their fifty-to-hundred-year lives. Design for 2050 climate conditions, not 1990 conditions. Build to higher standards than code requires—codes are minimums that lag reality. Integrate resilience from the start rather than value-engineering it out. And lead with resilience in your marketing—"storm-ready" and "climate-resilient" aren't just features, they're competitive advantages that attract buyers willing to pay premiums and who will be proven right over time.

For lenders, you are the linchpin. Integrate forward-looking climate risk into credit analysis, because historical loss rates are becoming less predictive. Require resilience standards as a condition of lending. Offer preferential rates for resilient properties—this rewards good behavior and mitigates your own risk. And rebuild specialized workout capabilities with people who understand climate-adjacent markets, because the convergence problems described in Chapter 9 are coming to more portfolios than anyone wants to admit.

For policymakers, implement dynamic risk mapping based on forward projections rather than historical data. Require climate risk disclosure in property transactions. Reform disaster recovery funding so it rewards pre-disaster mitigation rather than subsidizing repeated rebuilding in the same vulnerable locations. And stress test the system—not just individual banks, but the interconnected web of insurance, lending, property values, and infrastructure that determines whether communities survive or collapse.

Detailed action checklists for each of these stakeholder groups—organized by timeline and priority—are provided in the appendix.

The Bigger Picture

Everything I've outlined so far focuses on what individuals and organizations can do within the current system. But three systems need to evolve if we're going to navigate this convergence successfully.

The first is risk pricing and transfer. The current insurance model was designed for stationary climate conditions—a world where last year's loss data was a reasonable predictor of next year's risk. That world is gone. We need new mechanisms: parametric insurance that pays out automatically based on objective triggers—wind speed over 130 mph, rainfall over 10 inches, flood depth over 3 feet—rather than the glacial claims adjustment process. We need catastrophe bonds that transfer risk to capital markets rather than relying exclusively on traditional reinsurers, who themselves are concentrated and opaque. We need public-private risk pools that combine government backstops with private market discipline. And we need community-based insurance cooperatives that pool risk at local scales and align incentives for collective resilience. These mechanisms exist in nascent forms. They need to scale, fast.

The second is capital allocation and finance. The current financial system allocates capital based on backward-looking risk models and quarterly earnings cycles. We need mechanisms that price forward-looking climate risk into capital costs—so that assets in high-risk zones face higher borrowing costs, creating market pressure for adaptation or relocation. Patient capital that funds resilience retrofits should receive preferential treatment—lower rates, longer terms, favorable regulatory treatment. And when properties become unviable due to climate risk, we need mechanisms for managed retreat that don't trigger cascading financial failures. This is perhaps the hardest piece: how do you help communities relocate without destroying the wealth that's tied up in their real estate? The answer won't be simple, but avoiding the question is no longer an option.

The third is information and transparency. Markets cannot price risk they cannot see, and right now, too much climate risk is hidden. We need standardized climate risk disclosure for every property transaction—as routine as a title search or home inspection. We need open-source climate projection models accessible to anyone, not just institutional investors with Bloomberg terminals. We need real-time monitoring and early warning systems that track conditions as they evolve, not as they existed a decade ago. And we need full transparency on insurance costs and availability so that buyers understand the true total cost of ownership before they sign. The information infrastructure for climate-informed real estate decisions barely exists today. Building it is not optional—it's the foundation everything else rests on.

These are not small changes. But human beings are extraordinarily good at innovation when we must be. We went from the first airplane to landing on the moon in sixty-six years. We developed COVID vaccines in less than a year. We've made renewables cheaper than fossil fuels in most markets. When the incentives align and the stakes are clear, human ingenuity is extraordinary. The climate-real estate convergence creates exactly those conditions.

The Choice

I started this book with a storm metaphor. I told you about Hurricane Andrew, about watching from inland as it approached, about the choice people made between evacuating and staying.

Now, having worked through ten chapters of analysis and diagnosis, we return to the fundamental question: What choice will you make?

You can pretend the storm isn't coming. Continue operating as if yesterday's patterns will hold indefinitely. History suggests this won't work out well.

You can panic. Sell everything. Seek perfect safety in an uncertain world. This won't work either, because perfect safety doesn't exist and panic-driven decisions destroy value.

Or you can build resilience. Acknowledge the reality of what's happening—the debt cycle ending, climate volatility accelerating, systemic vulnerabilities accumulating—and respond strategically. Assess your exposure honestly. Diversify intelligently. Build absorption capacity through reserves and insurance. Create adaptive capacity through flexibility and optionality. Develop transformative capacity by innovating rather than just defending. And contribute to systemic resilience by strengthening the ecosystem you depend on.

This is the path forward. Not predicting the unpredictable but preparing for a range of outcomes. Not seeking certainty but building systems that can handle uncertainty.

A Final Word

When I started writing this book, people asked me: "Aren't you worried about scaring people?"

No. I'm worried about complacency. I'm worried about preventable catastrophes that happen because we were too comfortable to prepare. Fear is not the enemy. Complacency is.

My goal has never been to frighten you. It's been to help you see patterns that aren't obvious from inside the system, and to give you tools to respond.

The investors who reduced leverage and built reserves before the 2008 crisis didn't just avoid losses—they had capital to deploy when assets were selling at historic discounts. The developers who built Babcock Ranch didn't just survive Hurricane Ian—they proved a model that's now attracting premium buyers. The property owners who invested in resilience before insurance markets collapsed didn't just maintain coverage—they're now selling to buyers who can't get insurance elsewhere.

Resilience is not defensive. It is competitive advantage.

The storm is here. Not coming—here. The debt is maturing. The climate is volatile. The insurance markets are fragmenting. The banking system has vulnerabilities. But we are not helpless observers. We are active participants with the ability to shape outcomes.

The future belongs to those who saw clearly, prepared intelligently, and adapted decisively. Not to those who denied the changes happening around them. Not to those who panicked and made desperate decisions. To those who adjusted their sails.

The best time to build resilience was five years ago. The second-best time is today.

Pick one thing. One assessment to conduct, one reserve to build, one risk to mitigate, one conversation to have with a lender or insurer or partner. Do that one thing this week. Then next week, do another. Resilience isn't built in a single dramatic gesture. It's built through consistent, strategic choices over time. Each choice compounds. Each improvement strengthens the whole system.

You've spent hours reading this book, understanding the forces converging, learning from history, seeing the patterns and the fallacies. Now use that knowledge.

Build resilience in your portfolio. In your organization. In your community. In yourself.

You can't stop the wind. But you can adjust your sails.

That's resilience. That's survival. That's how we navigate together.

APPENDIX A
Sources and Further Reading

Climate Disasters and Frequency Data

NOAA National Centers for Environmental Information. "Billion-Dollar Weather and Climate Disasters" database (archived through 2024). ncei.noaa.gov/access/billions/

Climate Central. "2025 in Review: U.S. Billion-Dollar Disasters." January 2026.

Coastal Property Value Impacts

First Street Foundation. "Rising Seas Erode $15.8 Billion in Home Value from Maine to Mississippi." 2019.

Harvard Graduate School of Design. "Climate Gentrification: From Theory to Empiricism in Miami-Dade County." 2018.

UC Berkeley Haas School of Business. "Housing and Mortgage Markets with Climate Risk." Faculty Research.

Wildfires and Extreme Weather

Iglesias, V., et al. "Increasing Frequency and Intensity of the Most Extreme Wildfires on Earth." Nature Ecology & Evolution, vol. 8, 2024.

Arizona Department of Water Resources. "Phoenix AMA Groundwater Supply Updates." June 2023.

Iowa Flood Center, University of Iowa. "Iowa Flood Information and Research." iowafloodcenter.uiowa.edu

Insurance Market and Property Insurance

Citizens Property Insurance Corporation. "Policies in Force: Current Policy Count as of February 28, 2026." citizensfla.com

Bankrate. "Average homeowners insurance cost in March 2026." See also The Guardian, "California approves State Farm's request for 17% premium increase for homeowners," May 2025.

Sea Level Rise

Southeast Florida Regional Climate Change Compact. "Regionally Unified Sea Level Rise Projection" and 2024 guidance reaffirming use of the 2019 projection.

NOAA Office for Coastal Management. "Sea Level Rise Viewer." coast.noaa.gov/digitalcoast/tools/slr.html

Commercial Real Estate Debt

Mortgage Bankers Association. "Chart of the Week: Commercial Real Estate Loan Maturity Volumes." March 2026.

Mortgage Bankers Association. "2025 Commercial Real Estate Survey of Loan Maturity Volumes." Cited in MBA Newslink, March 2026.

Banking Regulation and Financial System Risk

Roosevelt Institute. "How 2018 Regulatory Rollbacks Set the Stage for the Silicon Valley Bank Collapse." 2023.

Barclay Damon. "The Dodd-Frank Banking Rule Rollback Explained." June 2018.

Private Equity and Systemic Risk

Stanford Graduate School of Business. "The Democratization of Private Equity Could Create a Systemic Risk Machine." 2024.

IMF. "Fast-Growing $2 Trillion Private Credit Market Warrants Closer Watch." IMF Blog, April 2024.

Federal Debt and National Security

Joint Economic Committee. "Monthly Debt Update." March 2026.

U.S. Treasury Fiscal Data. "Understanding the National Debt." fiscaldata.treasury.gov

Climate Resilience Projects

NPR. "Florida Community Designed to Weather Hurricanes Endured Ian With Barely a Scratch." October 2022.

ULI Developing Urban Resilience. Case studies: Babcock Ranch, The Wharf. developingresilience.uli.org

Historical Climate and Civilization

Sundberg, Adam. Natural Disaster at the Closing of the Dutch Golden Age: Floods, Worms, and the Cattle Plague. Cambridge University Press, 2022.

Economic Cycles and Theory

Dalio, Ray. Principles for Navigating Big Debt Crises. Bridgewater, 2018.

Dalio, Ray. The Changing World Order: Why Nations Succeed and Fail. Avid Reader Press, 2021.

Demographics and Generational Wealth

Pew Research Center. "Parents, Young Adult Children and the Transition to Adulthood." January 2024 (corrected April 2025).

Stanford Institute for Economic Policy Research / WFH Research. "Measuring Work from Home." 2025.

U.S. Census Bureau. "By 2030, All Baby Boomers Will Be Age 65 or Older." December 2019.

Zillow Research. "A 'Silver Tsunami' Won't Solve Housing Affordability Challenges." December 2024.

Rennison, Joe, and Julie Creswell. "Office Building Losses Start to Pile Up, and More Pain Is Expected." The New York Times, June 2024.

Galloway, Scott. "How the US is Destroying Young People's Future." TED Talk, 2024. See also: The Prof G Pod with Scott Galloway.

Reinsurance and Systemic Risk

International Association of Insurance Supervisors. "Reinsurance and Financial Stability." IAIS, July 2012.

Society of Actuaries. "Reviewing Systemic Risk within the Insurance Industry." SOA Research, February 2017.

Note: Sources and statistics in this appendix were refreshed through March 2026 where current data was available. For fast-moving figures, readers should consult Climate Central's continuation of the NOAA disasters series, FHFA, Freddie Mac, the U.S. Treasury, and their state insurance regulator for the latest updates. Also Subscribe to https://www.youtube.com/@billbymeldebtdoctor

• • •

A Practical Guide for Individual Property Owners

Immediate Actions (Next 30 Days):

- Assess your climate risk profile at FirstStreet.org. Get objective data on flood, fire, heat, and wind risk. Do not rely on outdated FEMA maps.

- Review your insurance coverage: renewal date, coverage limits, exclusions. If renewal is within six months and you're in a climate-vulnerable area, consider renewing early at current rates.

- Check refinancing dates. If debt matures within 24 months, start lender conversations now. Consider selling your property "subject to" your existing mortgage only with qualified legal and tax advice.

- Calculate absorption capacity. Can you handle a 50% insurance increase, a 2% rate jump, 3 months of vacancy? If not, begin building reserves immediately.

Medium-Term Actions (6–12 Months):

- Implement quick-win resilience improvements: weather stripping, gutter maintenance, tree trimming, securing outdoor items.
- Commission a resilience audit ($2,000–$5,000) for a prioritized list of vulnerabilities and improvements.
- Build reserve fund to 12 months of operating expenses and debt service.
- Reassess portfolio allocation for concentration risk.

Long-Term Actions (1–3 Years):

- Major upgrades: elevation, flood barriers, renewable energy, wildfire hardening.
- Transition floating or short-term debt to longer-term fixed rates.
- Consider geographic rebalancing if heavily concentrated in high-climate-risk areas.

For Real Estate Investors and Fund Managers

Implement climate stress testing across the full portfolio under multiple scenarios: 100-year flood, major wildfire season, Category 5 hurricane in each exposed region. Develop a resilience scorecard rating each asset on the four pillars. Set resilience targets alongside return targets. Integrate forward-looking climate projections—not just historical data—into underwriting. Build internal resilience expertise as a competitive advantage. Engage proactively with insurance markets. Invest in technology for monitoring and predictive maintenance. And be transparent with investors: frame resilience as value protection and competitive advantage, not overhead.

For Developers

Use climate projections for 2050–2075 conditions, not historical data. Build to higher standards than code requires. Integrate resilience from initial design rather than retrofitting. Obtain resilience certifications (LEED, WELL, Fortified Home, Enterprise Green Communities). Work with local government on area-wide resilience projects. Be the proof of concept that resilient development can be profitable.

For Policymakers and Regulators

Implement dynamic risk mapping incorporating real-time data and forward projections. Require climate risk disclosure in property transactions. Update building codes proactively using climate projections. Reform disaster recovery funding to incentivize pre-disaster mitigation. Provide tax incentives for resilience retrofits. Allow risk-based insurance pricing with means-tested subsidies for low-income households. Coordinate across agencies—climate adaptation, financial regulation, housing policy, and infrastructure investment cannot be siloed. Conduct system-wide stress tests modeling simultaneous climate events across regions.

For The Next Generation

The storm may cause some damage, but a new spring will arrive for you. Hang tight!